nudinits

Fun and Frolics in
Woolly Bush

By Sarah Simi

with knitting patterns by Caroline Bletsis

COLLINS & BROWN

Contents

Skill Levels
Depending on their difficulty, all the patterns have been labelled:

Soft easy for a beginner

Semi might need help

Hard will need an experienced hand

Join the villagers of Woolly Bush for fun and frolics as their Carnival comes to life!

Every summer the Woolly Bush Carnival is held in the village for everyone to have fun and all the traditional delights are there to be enjoyed. The vicar gets his maypole out, there's ring toss, a baking competition and a marrow growing contest, dog show, archery and animal showing featuring Jim's award-winning cock. Come and meet the villagers while they make woopee in Woolly Bush!

Everyone always crowds round to see Lady Fairisle's large opening and this year is no different – she starts proceedings by cutting the ribbon – let the fun begin!

The crowd had a lovely view of Lady Fairisle's big opening

The Big Opening

1
Entertainment
It's Showtime!

Fun Fact!

Dancing around a large upright pole was originally a fertility ritual although no-one knows why. In rural areas such as Woolly Bush a maypole was only up once a year but in more urban areas they had permanent wood, staying up all year.

Pole Dancing
The Maypole

Erected on the village green, every year the maypole gets the carnival underway. Robert the builder gives the vicar a hand getting it up and soon everyone is in position!

Everyone was enjoying

the vicar's erection

Barbara had never been a fan of pole dancing

Barbara thought someone
should have a fiddle

Lord Fairisle and Jim were about
to start beating very hard

9

Knocking Wood Together

Morris dancing

Either performed in front of the Ram Inn pub or on the village green, the Morris dancers are an essential part of the Woolly Bush Carnival with their bells, flowered hats, white hankies and long sticks. The usual formation is for at least four men to stand together, hold their wood up high and then knock them together. Although traditionally it was only men who were allowed to be Morris dancers, now plenty of women like to hold onto some wood while dancing.

The men held their wood in position

Bunting Pattern

Have it as long as you want!

Skill level
Soft

Finished size
Each flag is 4cm wide.

Materials
* Pair of 2.75mm knitting needles
* DK yarn in assorted colours for flags, small amounts
* White DK yarn for line, small amount
* 2.5mm crochet hook

Bunting flags
For each flag, cast on 8 sts in your chosen colour, leaving a 10cm tail of yarn for sewing.
Row 1: Knit.
Row 2: Purl.
Row 3: Knit.
Row 4: Purl.
Row 5: K1, ssk, k2, k2tog, k1. 6 sts
Row 6: Purl.
Row 7: K1, ssk, k2tog, k1. 4 sts
Row 8: Purl.
Row 9: Ssk, k2tog. 2sts
Row 10: Purl.
Row 11: K2tog and fasten off.
Weave in yarn end from cast-off sts.

Assembling the bunting
Using white DK yarn, crochet a chain the length you require for your bunting. If you can't crochet, weave in the ends of the cast-on yarn tails, then thread a length of yarn through the tops of the flags.

Using cast-on yarn tails, sew flags onto crochet chain, leaving 3 chain stitches between each flag and keeping the chain flat so that you sew all the flags on the same side. Weave in yarn ends through backs of flags.

Flower Pattern

Use these to decorate a Morris dancing hat or the top of a maypole – just cover a polystyrene ball with these beauties and you'll be ready to pole dance!

Skill level
Soft

Finished size (all flowers)
2.5–3.5cm wide

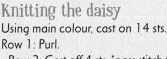

DAISY-TYPE FLOWER

Materials
* Pair of 2.75mm knitting needles
* DK yarn in main colour for petals, small amount
* DK yarn in contrast colour for flower centre, small amount
* Tapestry needle

Knitting the daisy
Using main colour, cast on 14 sts.
Row 1: Purl.
  Row 2: Cast off 4 sts, *pass stitch from right needle across to left needle, cast on 3 sts, cast off 4 sts*, repeat from * to * to last st. Cast off, leaving a tail of yarn for sewing.
  Thread yarn tail through cast-on stitches and pull tight to form a circle. Fasten off on back of work and weave in end.
  Using contrast colour, embroider a circle in backstitch in centre of flower at base

of petals, spiralling into the middle to fill up the circle. Fasten off on reverse and weave in end or leave yarn tail for sewing flower onto another item such as a hat.

SMALL FLOWER

Materials
* Pair of 2.75mm knitting needles
* DK yarn in main colour for petals, small amount
* DK yarn in contrast colour for flower centre, small amount
* Tapestry needle

Knitting the small flower
Using main colour, cast on 5 sts.
Row 1: Purl.
Row 2: (Kfbf) five times. 15 sts
Row 3: Purl.
  Row 4: Cast off 1 st, *pass stitch from right needle to left needle, cast on 1 st, cast off 4 sts*, rep from * to * to last 2 sts. Pass stitch from right needle across to left needle, cast on 1 st, cast off to end and fasten off.
  Cut yarn, leaving a tail of yarn for sewing. Thread yarn tail through cast-on stitches and pull tight to form a circle. Fasten off on back of work and weave in end.
  Using contrast colour, embroider three French knots close together in centre of

flower. Fasten off on reverse and weave in end or leave yarn tail for sewing flower onto another item such as a hat.

ROSE

Materials
✳ Pair of 2.75mm knitting needles
✳ DK yarn in main colour for flower, small amount
✳ DK yarn in green for base leaves, small amount
✳ Tapestry needle

Knitting the rose
Using main colour, cast on 30 sts, leaving yarn tail for sewing.

Rows 1–6: Work 6 rows in st st.

Cast off 4 sts, *swivel right needle around work clockwise (away from you) thus making yarn go around your work forming a scallop when pulled tight, then cast off another 4 sts. *Repeat from* to *until 6 sts left. Swivel needle one more time and cast off remaining 6 sts. Cut yarn, leaving a tail of yarn for sewing.

Roll work tightly from first 4 cast-off stitches, with cast-off edge being the top of the rose, and use cast-on yarn tail to sew through bottom of rose to hold roll secure throughout. Fasten off and weave in end. Using cast-off yarn tail, sew final large petal in place, pulling last cast-off stitch to base of flower. Secure and weave in end.

Knitting the base leaves
Using green yarn, cast on 9 sts.

Cast off 5 sts, *pass st on right needle across to left needle, cast on 4 sts, cast off 5 sts*. Repeat from * to * three more times. (Five leaves in total.) Cut yarn, leaving tail for sewing.

Thread yarn tail through base of all leaves (cast-on stitches) and pull tight, thus making leaves form a star shape. Sew to base of rose through centre of leaves and through each individual leaf to hold in place. Fasten off and weave in end or leave yarn tail for sewing rose to another item such as hat.

LEAVES

Materials
✳ Pair of 2.75mm knitting needles
✳ Green DK yarn, small amount
✳ Tapestry needle

Knitting the leaves
Cast on 1 st, leaving a 10cm tail of yarn for sewing.

Row 1: Kfbf. 3 sts

Row 2: Purl.

Row 3: K1, M1, k1, M1, k1. 5 sts

Rows 4–7: Beg with a P row, work 4 rows in st st.

Row 8: P2tog, p1, p2tog. 3 sts

Row 9: Knit.

Row 10: P3tog and fasten off.

Weave in end down centre of back of leaf.

Sew leaf in place using tail from cast-on st.

Note: Leaves can be knitted in different colours and sewn together at the base to make another kind of flower should you wish. Work French knots in a contrasting colour to form the centre.

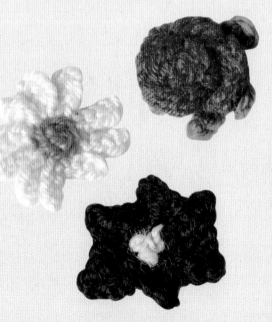

The Vicar's Organ

The vicar of St Angora's Church in Woolly Bush is the Rev Cecil Felting. He is a keen twitcher and likes nothing more than spending a few hours on Bushy Mound spotting a chiff chaff or a couple of hooters. He also enjoys foraging in Harden Forest, metal detecting in Bare Regis and Lindy Hop dancing.

He loves to play with his organ in the vestry but at the annual fete likes to entertain the crowds by bringing out his electric organ. His favourites to play are Onward Crocheted Soldiers and his own hit from the eighties, 'My Ding Dong Will Rise Once More'.

The vicar got the party going by playing with his organ

St Angora's
Church Fund

WE MADE IT!

THANK YOU

NEARLY THERE!

HALFWAY UP!

STARTING TO RISE!

RECTORY BUILDING
VESTRY FLASHING

TO DONATE PLEASE
CONTACT REV. CECIL FELTING

Raising funds for St Angora's church is something that the vicar spends lots of his time doing. One way he does this is to hold brass rubbing sessions in his rectory and the villagers are always eager to help out with any rubbing needed.

YARNAHA

BRASS RUBBING THIS W

The vicar and his accessories

The Rev Cecil Felting in all his glory, complete with his accessories of boots, dog collar and, of course, his binoculars for spotting all those tits!

Skill level
Hard

Finished size
The vicar is approx. 30cm tall.

Materials
* Pair of 2.75mm knitting needles
* One 100g ball of Sirdar Hayfield Bonus DK in Biscuit 963 for flesh
* Tapestry needle
* Stitch holder(s)
* 2 x 10mm glass eyes in blue
* Black wool for hair (we used black wool that has a little white running through it), small amount
* Pink embroidery thread, small amount
* Pink or red colouring pencil
* All-purpose glue
* Toy stuffing
* Quilt wadding, small amount
* 100 pack of 30cm white pipe cleaners
* 10cm polystyrene ball (preferably egg shaped) for the body
* 7cm polystyrene ball for the head
* Craft knife
* Sewing needle
* Templates (see note on page 95)
* Wire for glasses

THE VICAR

Knit all body parts in the same way as for Jim, using the flesh-coloured yarn – see page 80.

Making up the vicar

For materials, see page 14.
For templates, see page 95.

The method for assembling the vicar is essentially the same as for Jim (see page 83), apart from the hair. Embroider the hair on the vicar's head using black yarn and satin stitch, making long individual strands over the top of his head to create a combover. Embroider his eyebrows in straight stitch. For his chest, pubic and armpit hair, sew loops of yarn through the area and then cut and trim them so that you have short ends of yarn sticking out.

THE VICAR'S BINOCULARS

Skill Level
Semi

Finished size
4.5cm wide and 5cm long

Materials
* Stiff paper or thin card
* Sticky tape
* Clear plastic bag
* Pair of 2.75mm knitting needles
* Black DK yarn, small amount
* Tapestry needle
* Silver embroidery thread

This pattern involves a fair bit of improvisation! Many of the props I made for nudinits were from bits and pieces found that I around the house at the time and not necessarily anything that you might have to hand, so I have tried to make this pattern as easy to make as possible using everyday items.

Larger lenses – make 2
Cut two 4 x 5cm rectangles from card or paper. Roll into tubes 4cm long and 1.5cm in diameter and secure with sticky tape. Don't worry about how this looks – it will all get hidden eventually. Cut two circles 3cm in diameter from the plastic bag. Place one circle over one end of each tube and tape in place.

Using black yarn, cast on 12 sts.

Work in st st to the length of your tube, then cast off, leaving a tail of yarn for sewing.

Wrap the knitting around the tube. Using the yarn tail, overstitch the long ends of the tube together. (Again, don't worry about the appearance of the seam, as it will get hidden.)

Thread excess yarn through cast-on stitches at end of tube and gather gently until knitting slightly overlaps and hides the tube end. Fasten off and weave in ends. Repeat with cast-off stitches at other end of tube.

Smaller lenses – make 2
Cut two 2 x 4cm rectangles from card or paper. Roll into tubes 2cm long and 1cm in diameter and secure with sticky tape. Cut two circles 2cm in diameter from the plastic bag. Place one circle over one end of each tube and tape in place, as before.

Using black yarn, cast on 9 sts.

Work in st st for 2cm, then cast off, leaving a tail of yarn for sewing. Sew knitting around the tube, as before. Gather the end with the plastic circle, as before.

Assembling the binoculars
Insert one small lens tube into open end of a large lens tube, with 1cm poking out; make sure the plastic lens is on the outside of both tubes. Sew in place. Repeat with the remaining two tubes.

Sew the two completed tubes together, seams touching.

Wind silver embroidery thread tightly twice around larger end of each tube, fasten off and weave in ends. Do the same around ends of the smaller tubes.

Using black yarn, cast on 7 sts and work 3 rows in st st. Cast off, leaving a tail of yarn for sewing. Using one strand of silver embroidery thread, embroider the word 'YARNOX' across the strip. Sew strip across the centre of the two larger tubes.

Make another knitted strip, as above but without embroidery, and sew to bottom of binoculars.

Strap

Using black yarn and leaving a tail for sewing, cast on 3 sts and work garter stitch (all knit) to the desired length for your puppet – approx. 15cm. Cast off, leaving a tail of yarn for sewing.

Sew strap to either side of the larger tubes, at the end near the eyepiece. Using silver embroidery thread, stitch two straight stitches around the end of the strap, where it joins the binoculars, to resemble a metal loop.

THE VICAR'S DOG COLLAR

Materials

* Pair of 2.75mm knitting needles
* Black DK yarn, small amount
* White DK yarn, small amount

Making the dog collar
For the black part

Cast on 27 sts.
K11, cast off 5 sts, k to end.

Turn work. Working on these 11 sts only, work 3 rows in st st.

K11 sts and break off yarn, leaving a long end. Attach main ball of yarn to sts

on left-hand needle. Work 3 rows in st st.

Cast on 5 sts using the long end of yarn.

Knit across the cast-on sts and rest of the row with the wool from the main ball.

Cast off.

Weave in any loose ends.

For the white part

Cast on 6 sts.
Work 5 rows in st st.
Cast off, leaving a tail of yarn.
Weave in the cast-on tail.

Making up the collar

Fold the white section in half, wrong sides together and aligning the cast-on and cast-off edges. Sew the cast-on and cast-off edges together.

Fold the black section in half lengthways, wrong sides together and aligning the cast-on and cast-off edges. Start to sew the edges together. When you get near the centre, place the folded white section into the collar, so that the white sticks through. Catch this down with a couple of stitches to hold. Carry on sewing the edges of the collar together.

Sew the short ends together when the collar is placed around the vicar's neck.

THE VICAR'S GLASSES

Materials

* Wire
* Template (see note on page 95)
* Grey or silver yarn, small amount
* All-purpose glue

Making the glasses

Bend wire into the shape of the glasses, following the template.

Glue the end of the grey or silver yarn onto one end of the glasses. Wind yarn tightly around the wire. Hold the tension while you glue down the yarn when you reach the other end. Leave to dry, then trim off excess yarn.

THE VICAR'S BOOTS

Skill level
Soft

Finished size
7cm long

Materials
* Pair of 3mm knitting needles
* Dark brown DK yarn, small amount
* Tapestry needle
* Template (see note on page 95)
* Black felt
* Yellow or orange laceweight or baby yarn, small amount
* Tweed DK yarn (black-and-grey mix), small amount
* 3mm crochet hook

Boots – make 2
Using dark brown yarn, cast on 45 sts.
Row 1: Purl.
Row 2: Knit.
Row 3: Purl.
Row 4: Knit.
Row 5: Purl.
Row 6: K20, ssk, k1, k2tog, k20. 43 sts
Row 7: P19, p2tog, p1, p2tog, p19. 41 sts
Row 8: K18, ssk, k1, k2tog, k18. 39 sts
Row 9: P17, p2tog, p1, p2tog, p17. 37 sts
Row 10: K16, ssk, k1, k2tog, k16. 35 sts
Row 11: P15, p2tog, p1, p2tog, p15. 33 sts
Row 12: K14, turn.
Row 13: Cast on 2 sts and p16 (work on these 16 sts only).
Rows 14–18: Work 5 rows in st st. Cast off.
Row 19: Rejoin yarn to remaining sts, k5, turn (work on these 5 sts only).
Rows 20–24: Work 5 rows in st st. Cast off.
Row 25: Rejoin yarn to remaining 14 sts, cast on 2 sts, k16.
Rows 26–30: Work 5 rows in st st.
Cast off, leaving a long tail of yarn for sewing.

Making up the boots
Fold boot in half lengthways, wrong sides together, and sew back seam.

Using the template, cut out the boot sole in black felt and pin to bottom of knitted boot. Sew together using blanket stitch. The knitted part may look too big for the sole, but you will be able to ease the sole in if you sew through each cast-on stitch as you go.

Cut a long length of dark brown yarn and blanket stitch around all edges of the top of the boot, including the tongue; this tidies up the edges and keeps the boot's shape.

Laces – make 2
Using black laceweight or baby yarn, crochet a 15cm length of chain and weave in ends. Using a tapestry needle, sew the laces in place as you would lace up a real shoe.

'Socks' – make 2
Using tweed yarn, cast on 30 sts. Check that 30 sts is the right length to fit around your puppet's ankle – it depends on the yarn you are using. Adjust the number of stitches accordingly, if necessary, but make sure you have an even number of stitches.
Row 1: K1, p1 to end.
Cont in rib for 3cm.
Cast off, leaving a tail of yarn for sewing.

Fold in half lengthways, right sides together, and stitch long edges together to make a tube. Slip tube over puppet's leg, then slip boot over the top. Roll down top edge of 'sock' to meet top of boot; sew in place if necessary.

2
Competitions
Big Dongs!

Pattie was showing
off her poodle

Jim's Willie was after
Joan's Growler

Doggies in Position

Who will come first in the dog show?
There's a prize for waggiest tail and
best-groomed pooch. Jim's Willie
usually makes a late entry!

Willie
(Kennel Club name
'Fabulous Willie')
Border Collie
owned by Jim
McFurry

Growler
Lurcher cross
owned by Joan
Fleece

Prince Albert
(Kennel Club name
'The Nelson's Head
at Friday Night')
Deerhound owned by
Lord Fairisle

Nippy
(Kennel Club name
'It's A Bit Nippy
Out') Miniature
poodle owned by
Hattie & Pattie

Rodger
Terrier
cross owned by
Robert Argyle

A Taste
Of
Barbara's
Pantry

Pattern for Jim's Willie

Jim's faithful companion Willie – he's not always well behaved!

Skill level
Hard

Finished size
Willie is 16cm long and 12cm tall.

Materials
* Pair of 3mm knitting needles
* One 100g ball of black DK yarn
* One 100g ball of white DK yarn
* Soft eyelash yarn in white and black, small amounts
* Tapestry needle
* 2 x 6mm brown safety eyes
* Black embroidery thread
* Kapok stuffing
* Length of narrow ribbon in colour of choice for collar
* Small metal bell or disc (optional)

Body and Head, Side 1
Using black yarn, cast on 8 sts.
Row 1: (Kfb) eight times. 16 sts
Row 2: Purl.
Row 3: K2, (kfb, k1) to last 2 sts, k2. 22 sts
Row 4: Purl.
Row 5: Kfb, k20, kfb. 24 sts
Row 6: Purl.
Row 7: K23, kfb. 25 sts
Row 8: Join white yarn. P2 white, p23 black.
Row 9: K23 black, k2 white.
Row 10: P3 white, p22 black.
Row 11: K22 black, k2 white, kfb white. 26 sts
Row 12: P3 white, p23 black.
Row 13: K23 black, k3 white.
Row 14: P3 white, p23 black.
Row 15: K2tog black, k22 black, k2 white. 25 sts
Row 16: P1 white, cut white yarn and weave in end as you go, p24 black.
Row 17: K2tog, k22. 24 sts
Row 18: Purl.
Row 19: Cast off 14 sts, k to end. 10 sts
Row 20: Purl.
Row 21: Knit.
Row 22: Purl.
Row 23: Cast on 4 sts, p to end. 14 sts
Row 24: K2tog, (kfb, k1) to last 4 sts, k4. 17 sts
Rows 25–28: Work 4 rows in st st.
Row 29: P2tog, p15. 16 sts
Row 30: K12, join white yarn, k2 white, k2tog white. 15 sts
Row 31: Cast off 4 sts in white, p1 white, p10 black. 11 sts
Row 32: K9 black, k2 white.
Row 33: P2tog white, p1 white, in black (p2tog, p1) twice, p2tog. 7 sts
Row 34: K5 black, k2 white.
Cast off in black, p2tog at either end.

Body and Head, Side 2
Rows 1–6: Work as Side 1.
Row 7: Kfb, k23. 25 sts
Row 8: P23 black, join white yarn, p2 white.
Row 9: K2 white, k23 black,
Row 10: P22 black, p3 white.
Row 11: Kfb white, k2 white, k22 black. 26 sts
Row 12: P23 black, p3 white.
Row 13: K3 white, k23 black.
Row 14: P23 black, p3 white.
Row 15: K2 white, k22 black, k2tog black. 25 sts
Row 16: P24 black, p1 white. Cut white yarn and weave in end as you go.
Row 17: K22, k2tog. 24 sts
Row 18: Purl.
Row 19: Knit.
Row 20: Cast off 14 sts, p to end. 10 sts
Rows 21–24: Work 4 rows in st st.
Row 25: Cast on 4 sts, k to end. 14 sts
Row 26: Purl.
Row 27: K4, (kfb, k1) to last 2 sts, k2tog. 17 sts
Rows 28–30: Work 3 rows in st st.

Row 31: K2tog, k15. 16 sts
Row 32: P12, join white yarn, p2 white, p2tog white. 15 sts
Row 33: Cast off 4 sts in white, k1 white, k10 black. 11 sts
Row 34: P9 black, p2 white.
Row 35: K2tog white, k1 white, in black (k2tog, k1) twice, k2tog. 7 sts
Row 36: P5 black, p2 white.
Cast off in black, k2tog at either end.

Making up the body and head

Place sides 1 and 2 right sides together and sew from end of cast-on stitches, up chest to head and around body to other end of cast-on stitches, using white yarn for the white chest and face seams and black yarn for rest of head and body. Do not cut black yarn at the gap yet.

Turn right side out. Attach eyes either side of white blaze on face. Stuff head and body firmly, keeping a natural shape – particularly on the head. Sew up the gap.

Using all six strands of black embroidery thread, sew the nose by working straight horizontal stitches in a triangular shape at end of muzzle. Make one stitch downwards from middle of base of nose, about 5mm long. Insert needle where you want the end of the mouth to be, make a long stitch across muzzle behind the downward stitch and bring needle out where the other side of the mouth should

be. Pull gently to form mouth, then pass needle to base of head and fasten off, weaving in thread ends.

Using white eyelash yarn, sew several small stitches among white chest blaze, fasten off and weave in ends. Tease out strands carefully with a needle or a toothbrush.

Ears – make 2

Using black DK yarn, cast on 7 sts, leaving a tail of yarn for sewing.
Rows 1–6: Beg with a k row, work 6 rows in st st.

Row 7: (K1, k2tog) twice, k1. 5 sts
Row 8: Purl.
Row 9: K2tog, k1, k2tog. 3 sts
Row 10: Purl.
Row 11: K3tog and fasten off. Weave in end.

Using cast-on yarn tail, sew ear to head, curving the base slightly. Fold ear forwards in a natural way and hold in place with a stitch or two if necessary. Sew a couple of stitches of white eyelash yarn into the ear to create some fluff.

Tail

Using black yarn, cast on 7 sts.
Work 3cm in st st, ending with a p row.
Change to white yarn and work 2 more
rows in st st.
Next row: K2tog, k3, k2tog. 5 sts
Next row: K1, k2tog, k2. 4 sts
Next row: Purl.
Next row: K2tog, k2. 3 sts
Next row: P3tog and fasten off.

Fold tail in half lengthways, wrong sides
together, and sew along long edge, using
white yarn for the white part and black
yarn for the black part. Do not close cast-
on edge. Sew tail to dog's body in centre
of his bottom, keeping the seam side
down. Using eyelash yarn, make a few
stitches in black up black part of seam
and a few stitches in white up white part
of seam. Fasten off and weave in ends.
Tease out strands carefully, as before.

Front legs - make 2

Using white yarn, cast on 4 sts, leaving a
  tail of yarn for sewing.
Row 1: (Kfb) four times. 8 sts
Row 2: Purl.
Row 3: (Kfb) eight times. 16 sts
Row 4: Purl.
Row 5: K6, (k2tog) twice, k6. 14 sts
Row 6: P5, (p2tog) twice, p5. 12 sts
Row 7: K4, (k2tog) twice, k4. 10 sts
Row 8: Purl.

Rows 9–16: Change to black yarn,
  leaving a yarn tail for sewing. Work 8
  rows in st st.
Row 17: (Kfb, k2, kfb, k1) twice. 14 sts
Rows 18–24: Work 7 rows in st st.
Row 25: (K2tog, k4) twice, k2tog. 11 sts
Cast off, p2tog at either end.

Fold leg in half lengthways, wrong sides
together, and sew from the foot upwards
using yarn tails to do so. Leave cast-
off edge open and stuff leg carefully,
keeping the stuffing firm but the shape
natural. Sew up the gap. Using black
yarn, sew four small vertical stitches on
front of foot for claws.

Attach front legs using same method as
for the pig (see page 38).

Back legs - make 2

Rows 1–8: Work as for
  front legs.
Rows 9–18: Change
  to black yarn. Work
  10 rows in st st.
Row 19: Kfb, k3, (kfb) twice,
  k3, kfb1. 14 sts
Row 20: Purl.
Row 21: K6, (kfb) twice, k6.
  16 sts
Rows 22–28: Work 7 rows
  in st st.
Row 29: K7, k2tog, k7.
  15 sts

Row 30: P2tog, p3, (p2tog) twice, p3,
  p2tog, p1. 11 sts
Cast off, k2tog at either end.
Sew, stuff and add claws, as for front legs.

Attach back legs using method as for
the pig (see page 38).

Using black eyelash yarn, stitch several
small stiches up the black seam of the
back legs, fasten, then tease out the
strands as before.

Make a collar with the ribbon, cutting it
to size and sewing it onto the dog. Add a
small metal bell or disc if you wish.

Are you a grower or a shower?

Marrow Competition

The Woolly Bush Marrow Growers Association was established in 1930 by Ivor Biggin. The members are very secretive about how to grow a real whopper, there are fabled stories of feeding the plants Ballmers cider in order to make them bigger but in reality this only makes them droopy. Size really is everything in this competition and the biggest always wins!

Lady Fairisle presented Bernard with a trophy for having the biggest one

WOOLLY BUSH
MARROW GROWERS
SOCIETY
WE LIKE HAVING IT STUFFED

Soggy Bottom

The Great Woolly Bush Bake Off is held every year in the Village Hall. The judges are identical twins Hattie and Pattie – Hattie runs Hattie's Cakes and Pattie runs Pattie's Bakes, shops next to one another on Woolly Bush High Street. The competition this year is for the best sponge cake with entrants eager to show off their red velvet!

Barbara was soaking her black forest

INDEKNIT

The vicar took first prize with his showstopper

Hattie/Pattie and accessories

Easy to make, difficult to tell apart! Hattie and Pattie have their own lacy scarf and different-coloured shoes, so you know who's who!

Skill level
Hard

Finished size
Hattie/Pattie is approx. 28cm tall.

Materials
* Pair of 2.75mm knitting needles
* One 100g ball of Sirdar Hayfield Bonus DK in Biscuit 963 for flesh tones
* Tapestry needle
* Stitch holder(s)
* Templates (see note on page 95)
* Craft knife
* 10cm polystyrene ball (preferably egg shaped) for the body
* 7cm polystyrene ball for the head
* Pack of 100 30cm white pipe cleaners
* Sticky tape
* Quilt wadding, small amount
* Toy stuffing
* 2 x 10mm glass eyes in green
* All-purpose glue
* Light brown yarn for hair, small amount
* Pink embroidery thread, small amount
* Embroidery needle
* Hair-coloured sewing thread and sewing needle
* Pink or red colouring pencil

TO MAKE HATTIE/PATTIE

Using flesh-coloured yarn, work in the same way as for Jim (see page 80), apart from the changes to legs and body described below. (There's no need to knit a willy either!)

Legs - make 2

Work the same way as for Jim (see page 80), but cast off after row 44.

Front of body

Rows 1–17: Work as for Jim (see page 80). 34 sts
Rows 18–20: Beg with a K row, work 3 rows in st st, dec 1 st at each end of every row. 28 sts
Row 21: Purl.
Row 22–27: Beg with a K row, work 6 rows in st st, dec 1 st at each end of every knit row. 22 sts
Row 28–35: Beg with a K row, work 8 rows in st st, inc 1 st at each end of every knit row. 30 sts
Row 36–39: Beg with a K row, work 3 rows in st st, dec 1 st at each end of every knit row. 26 sts
Rows 40–42: Beg with a K row, work 3 rows in st st, dec 1 st at each of every row. 20 sts
Row 43: Purl.
Row 44: Dec 1 st at each end of row. 18 sts
Row 45: Purl.
Row 46–48: Beg with a K row, work 3 rows in st st, dec 1 st at each end of every K row. 12 sts
Row 49: Purl.
Cast off.

Back of body

Rows 1–17: Work as for Jim (see page 80).
Rows 18–19: Beg with a K row, work 2 rows in st st, dec 1 st at each end of every row. 30 sts
Rows 20–25: Beg with a K row, work 6 rows in st st, dec 1 st at each end of every K row. 24 sts
Rows 26–39: Beg with a K row, work 14 rows in st st, dec 1 st at each end of last row. 22 sts
Row 40: Purl.
Rows 41–45: Beg with a K row, work 5 rows in st st, dec 1 st at each end of every row. 12 sts
Row 46: Purl.
Rows 47–48: Beg with a K row, work 2 rows in st st.
Cast off.

Making up Hattie/Pattie

The method for assembling Hattie/Pattie is essentially the same as for Jim (see page 83), but the body pieces are shaped to create a waist and boobs, so you'll need to add extra stuffing.

In order to get more shape in the chest, start a small running stitch from under one armpit up into the cleavage and then back around to the other armpit, pulling as you go. Secure tightly.

For the hair, loop light brown yarn around your hand until you have enough to cover the head. To create a parting, stitch the yarn down the centre of the head with embroidery thread, bring the yarn round on either side to the back of the head and sew down again with embroidery thread. Plait a thin strand of yarn, place it around the head and secure with thread. Plait a thicker amount, twist it into a bun shape and stitch to the back of the head. With a small amount of yarn, create a swirl for the front of the head and catch down with thread. You can add one of the flowers from page 10 on one side if you wish.

You may need to press the scarf with an iron to stop it from curling.

SCARF

Skill level
Hard

Materials
* Pair of 2.75mm knitting needles
* White baby yarn (small amount)
* Narrow ribbon in colour of choice (small amount)

To make the scarf
Cast on 8 sts.
Row 1: Purl.
Row 2: *Yo, k2, yo, k2, k2tog, yo, k1, p1.
Row 3: K1, p6, yo, k2tog, p1.
Row 4: Yo, k2, yo, k4, k2tog, yo, k1, p1.
Row 5: K1, p8, yop, k2tog, p1.

Row 6: Yo, k2, yo, k6, k2tog, yo, k1, p1.
Row 7: K1, p7, k2tog, yo, (k2tog) twice.
Row 8: Yo, k2tog, k1, yo, k2tog, k3, k2tog, yo, k1, p1.
Row 9: K1, p5, k2tog, yo, k2tog, (k2tog) twice.
Row 10: Yo, k2tog, k1, yo, k2tog, k1, k2tog, yo, k1, p1.
Row 11: K1, p3, k2tog, yo, k2tog, k2tog*.
Rep rows 2–11 eight times.
Cast off and weave in ends. Thread ribbon through the holes along the flat edge of the scarf.
Tie the scarf in a bow around the neck of your puppet and cut off the excess ribbon.

CAMEO BROOCH

Skill level
Soft

Materials
* Brown felt, small amount
* White baby yarn, small amount
* White embroidery thread
* Embroidery needle
* Hook-and-loop tape (optional)

To make the brooch
Cut two identical ovals of brown felt, 2 cm long. Place them together and, using white baby yarn, sew together using blanket stitch, keeping the stitches slightly loose to form a scalloped border all around the brooch.

Using two strands of white embroidery thread, embroider the shape of a face in profile in the centre of the brooch.

Place the brooch in the centre of the bow of the scarf. You can either sew it in place or, if you want it to be removeable, use a small piece of hook-and-loop tape.

If you are attaching the cameo, bring the ribbon ends to the back of the puppets neck and tuck under the scarf.

PATTIE/HATTIE'S SHOES

Skill level
Soft

Finished size
6.5cm long

Materials
✳ Pair of 3mm knitting needles
✳ Light or dark brown DK yarn, small amount
✳ Tapestry needle
✳ Template (see note on page 95)
✳ Black felt, small amount
✳ Gold embroidery thread, small amount
✳ Embroidery needle

Shoe upper – make 2
Cast on 45 sts.
Rows 1–5: Starting with a P row, work 5 rows in st st.
Row 6: K20, ssk, k1, k2tog, k20. 43 sts
Row 7: P19, p2tog, p1, p2tog, p19. 41 sts
Row 8: K18, ssk, k1, k2tog, k18. 39 sts
Row 9: P17, p2tog, p1, p2tog, p17. 37 sts
Row 10: K16, ssk, k1, k2tog, k16. 35 sts
Row 11: Cast off 15 sts, p4 (so you will end up with 5 sts, including 1 already on right-hand needle), cast off remaining 15 sts and cut yarn, leaving a long tail for sewing.
Row 12: Rejoin yarn, k to end.
Row 13: Purl.
Row 14: K2tog, k1, k2tog. 3 sts
Cast off, leaving a 30cm tail of yarn.

Making up the shoe
With tapestry needle, thread yarn to base of shoe tongue, then blanket stitch all around edge of tongue. Weave in ends.

With right sides together, using yarn tail from cast-off edge, sew back seam of shoe upper.

Using shoe template, cut out sole of shoe in black felt. Pin shoe upper to sole at toe and heel. Using same yarn as for shoe, blanket stitch upper to sole all around. The knitted shoe will seem too large for the sole, but as you sew it will form a solid edge and fit nicely.

Using all six strands of gold embroidery thread, stitch two or three 1cm stitches across base of shoe tongue to make a bar. Alternatively, if you are feeling fancy, use gold ribbon to make a buckle!

Victoria sponge

A British classic - soft sponges covered in cream, just how Bernard likes it! Use different-coloured yarns to make different cakes from the same pattern - try a red velvet or a coffee and walnut!

Skill level
Semi

Finished size
The Victoria sponge is 5.5cm in diameter.

Materials
* Set of four 2.75mm double-pointed knitting needles (dpns)
* Light brown DK yarn, small amount
* Kapok stuffing
* Crimson DK yarn, small amount
* White baby yarn, small amount
* Tapestry needle

Sponge cake - make 2
Using light brown yarn, cast on 3 sts.
Round 1: (Kfb) three times. Divide stitches evenly between 3 dpns and join to work in the round. 6 sts
Round 2: (Kfb, k1) three times. 9 sts
Round 3: (Kfb, k2) three times. 12 sts
Round 4: (Kfb, k3) three times. 15 sts
Round 5: (Kfb, k4) three times. 18 sts
Round 6: (Kfb, k2) six times. 24 sts
Round 7: Knit.
Round 8: (Kfb, k3) six times. 30 sts
Round 9: Knit.
Round 10: (Kfb, k4) six times. 36 sts
Round 11: Knit.
Round 12: Purl.
Round 13: Knit.
Round 14: Knit.
Round 15: Knit.
Round 16: Purl.
Round 17: Knit.
Round 18: (K2tog, k4) six times. 30 sts
Round 19: Knit.
Round 20: (K2tog, k3) six times. 24 sts
Round 21: Knit.
Round 22: (K2tog, k2) six times. 18 sts
Round 23: (K2tog, k4) three times. 15 sts
Round 24: (K2tog, k3) three times. 12 sts
Stuff with just enough stuffing to fill the cake lightly and still keep a flat shape.
Round 25: (K2tog, k2) three times. 9 sts
Round 26: (K2tog, k1) three times. 6 sts
Cut yarn, leaving a 10cm tail for sewing.

Thread yarn tail through stitches on your needles, pull tight and fasten. This may form a small bump – pass yarn through centre of cake to the other side, pull until bump flattens and fasten off. Weave in ends.

Jam filling
Using crimson yarn, cast on 3 sts.
  Rounds 1–11: Work as for sponge cake pattern.
  Cast off, leaving a 20cm tail for sewing. Join last cast-off stitch to first cast-off stitch to tidy up the edge. Sew jam in place on one of the cakes.
  Using brown yarn, carefully sew cakes together with jam in centre, pulling yarn through all three layers from top to bottom all around edge of cake. Pull each stitch just tight enough to keep cake flat – not too tight or it will form dents.

Icing
Using white baby yarn, cast on 3 sts.
  Rounds 1–11: Work as for sponge cake pattern.
  Round 12: (Kfb, k5) six times. 42 sts
  Round 13: Knit.
  Cast off, leaving a 30cm tail for sewing. Join last cast-off stitch to first cast-off stitch to tidy up edge. Sew icing to top of cake, using raised purl row as a guide.
  Using red yarn, embroider French knots all around edge of icing and in the centre,

making sure you sew through both the icing and the top layer of the cake, as this also serves to keep the icing flat.

Note: You can make different cakes by using a different-coloured yarn – dark brown for a chocolate cake, a white centre instead of red for cream instead of jam, etc.

Fairy cake

A couple of mouthfuls and a cherry on top – perfect!

Skill level
Semi

Finished size
The fairy inccake is 3.5cm in diameter.

Materials
* Set of four 2.75mm double-pointed knitting needles (dpns)
* DK yarn in light brown or dark brown (depending on flavour!), small amount
* DK yarn in pastel colours for icing, small amounts
* DK in crimson for cherry, small amount
* Kapok stuffing
* Tapestry needle
* Beads and embroidery thread (optional)

Cake
Using brown yarn, cast on 3 sts.
Round 1: (Kfb) three times. Divide stitches evenly between 3 dpns and join to work in the round. 6 sts
Round 2: (Kfb, k1) three times. 9 sts
Round 3: (Kfb, k2) three times. 12 sts
Round 4: (Kfb, k3) three times. 15 sts
Round 5: Knit.
Round 6: Purl.
Round 7: (Kfb, k2) five times. 20 sts
Round 8: (K1, p1) ten times. 20 sts
Rounds 9–12: Rep round 8.
Round 13: P6, pfb, p6, pfb, p5, pfb. 23 sts
Round 14: Purl.
Round 15: Knit.
Round 16: K2tog, k6, k2tog, k6, k2tog, k5. 20 sts
Rounds 17–21: Knit.
Cast off, leaving a tail of yarn for sewing. Join last cast-off stitch to first cast-off stitch to tidy up the edge. Fold work at top of double purl round, pushing the knit section into the rib section to make a firm cake base. Sew cast-off edge to edge of base, using single purl round as a guide. Weave in ends.

Icing

Using your chosen colour, cast on 40 sts.
  Row 1: Purl.

  Cast off, leaving a 30cm yarn tail for sewing. Sew strip into a conical spiral, then sew outer edge of icing to cake base at the edge, just inside double purl row, leaving a small gap; do not fasten off. Stuff cake through the gap, taking care not to over-stuff it, and shape base and icing. Sew up gap and weave in ends.

Cherry

Using crimson yarn, cast on 4 sts.
Row 1: (Kfb) four times. 8 sts
Row 2: Purl.
Row 3: (K2tog) four times. 4 sts
  Cast off, leaving a 20cm yarn tail for sewing. Thread yarn through sts on needle and make small running stitches around rest of work. Pull together tightly to form a small ball and fasten; do not cut yarn. Sew cherry to top of icing cone, pull yarn through cake, catch a small stitch of the base and pass yarn back up to cherry. Pull gently until base is nice and flat and the stitches are hidden. Continue to sew cherry with a couple more stitches and fasten off.

Note: The icing can also be decorated with small beads as 'sprinkles' or embroidery — let your imagination go!

Mixing bowl

Hold this and something is bound to go stiff.

- - - - - - - - -

Skill level
Soft

Finished size
The mixing bowl is 7cm in diameter.

Materials
* Set of four 3mm double-pointed knitting needles (dpns)
* Light brown DK yarn, small amount
* Cream/white DK yarn, small amount
* Tapestry needle
* Fabric stiffener (optional)

Using light brown yarn, cast on 6 sts.
  Divide sts evenly between 3 dpns and join to work in the round.
Round 1: (Kfb, k1) three times. 9 sts
Round 2: (Kfb, k2) three times. 12 sts
Round 3: (Kfb, k3) three times. 15 sts
Round 4: (Kfb, k4) three times. 18 sts
Rounds 5–6: Purl.
Round 7: (Kfb, k1) nine times. 27 sts
Round 8: Knit.

Round 9: (Kfb, k2) nine times. 36 sts
Rounds 10–11: Knit.
Round 12: (Kfb, k5) six times. 42 sts
Rounds 13–19: Knit.
Rounds 14–15: Purl.
Round 16: Join cream/white yarn and cut brown. Knit to end, weaving in ends as you go.
Rounds 17–23: Knit.
Round 24: (K2tog, k5) six times. 36 sts
Round 25: Knit.
Round 26: (K2tog, k2) nine times. 27 sts
Round 27: Knit.
Round 28: (K2tog, k1) nine times. 18 sts
Round 29: (K2tog, k4) three times. 15 sts
Round 30: (K2tog, k3) three times. 12 sts
Round 31: (K2tog) six times. 6 sts
  Cut yarn, thread through the 6 sts and draw tight. Fasten off, but do not cut yarn. Push cream/white section inside brown section to form bowl and sew in place with small stitches around base through both layers of work. Weave in ends.

  Using light brown yarn, embroider a pattern around the outside — this is made with two bracket-shaped stitches, each caught in centre with a tiny running stitch, spaced out around bowl.

  Using cream/white yarn, thread a length of yarn between the two layers at top rim of bowl and gently pull until rim is the right circumference. Fasten off and weave in ends.

If you would like your bowl to be a little harder, apply fabric stiffener generously to the inside layer, shape carefully and leave to dry.

Wooden spoon

Beat it as hard as you can.

Skill level
Soft

Finished size
The spoon is 10cm long.

Materials
* Pair of 2.75mm knitting needles
* Mid-brown DK yarn, small amount
* Kebab stick
* Tacky glue
* Tapestry needle

Spoon handle
Cut kebab stick to 10cm in length, discarding sharp end.

Coat stick with tacky glue and wrap tightly with brown yarn. Don't worry if one end is untidy, as this will be hidden in the bowl of the spoon.

Spoon bowl
Cast on 3 sts.
Row 1: Purl.
*Row 2: Kfb, k1, kfb. 5 sts
Row 3: Purl.
Row 4: Kfb, k3, kfb. 7 sts
Row 5: Purl.
Row 6: Kfb, k5, kfb. 9 sts
Rows 7–9: Beg with a P row, work 3 rows in st st.
Row 10: K2tog, k5, k2tog. 7 sts
Row 11: Purl.

Row 12: K2tog, k3, k2tog. 5 sts
Row 13: Purl.
Row 14: K2tog, k1, k2tog*. 3 sts
Row 15: Purl.
Repeat from * to *, then cast off, leaving a long tail of yarn for sewing.

Making up the spoon
Fold work at centre row, right sides together, and sew all round, leaving cast-on/cast-off edges open. Do not cut yarn. Turn right side out and insert untidy end of spoon handle into bowl. Sew cast-on/cast-off edges closed around handle, then sew running stitches around edge of bowl, just below ridge made by inner seam, pulling gently as you go to create a curve and dip in the spoon. Fasten off and weave in any ends.

Best Cock in Show

Jim is the local farmer in Woolly Bush and he likes to show his animals during the carnival. He spends the weeks leading up to the show washing and brushing them till they look the best they can be — his cock is always a highlight!

Jim was showing Barbara how natural his semi was

Barbara was delighted Jim's cock had come first

Pig, piglets and poo

A rare breed Woollenshire Old Spot mother piggy. Her udders are made of poppers and the piglets snap straight on to feed!

Skill level
Hard

Finished size
Mother pig: 18cm long, 11cm tall
Piglets: 9cm long, 5cm tall

Materials
* Pair of 3mm knitting needles
* Set of four 2.75mm double-pointed knitting needles (dpns)
* One 100g ball of pink DK yarn
* One 100g ball of black DK yarn
* Camouflage green or brown DK yarn for the poo, small amount
* Kapok stuffing
* Tapestry needle
* 2 x 6mm brown safety eyes for pig
* 2 x 4mm brown safety eyes for each piglet
* 6 snap fasteners (poppers)
* Pink sewing thread
* Sewing needle

MOTHER PIG

Body
Using pink yarn, cast on 12 sts.
Row 1: Knit.
Row 2: Purl.
Row 3: (Kfb) twice, k2, (kfb) four times, k2, (kfb) twice. 20 sts
Row 4: Purl.
Row 5: (Kfb, k1) twice, k2, (kfb, k1) four times, k2, (kfb, k1) twice. 28 sts
Row 6: Purl.
Row 7: (Kfb, k2) twice, k2, (kfb, k2) four times, k2, (kfb, k2) twice. 36 sts
Row 8: Purl.
Row 9: (Kfb, k3) twice, K2, (kfb, k3) four times, k2, (kfb, k3) twice. 44 sts
Row 10: Purl.
Row 11: Knit.
Row 12: Purl.
Row 13: Knit.
Row 14: Purl.
Row 15: K31, join black, k2 black, k11 pink.
Row 16: P10 pink, p4 black, p30 pink.
Row 17: K30 pink, k4 black, k10 pink.
Row 18: P11 pink, p2 black, p31 pink, carrying black yarn along behind work for a further 13 sts.
Row 19: K15 pink, k3 black, k26 pink.
Row 20: P25 pink, p5 black, p14 pink.
Row 21: K13 pink, k7 black, k24 pink.
Row 22: P23 pink, p9 black, p12 pink.
Row 23: K12 pink, k9 black, carrying black yarn across along behind work as you k11 pink, k3 black, k9 pink.
Row 24: P8 pink, p5 black, p11 pink, p9 black, p12 pink.
Row 25: K12 pink, k9 black, k10 pink, k6 black, k7 pink.
Row 26: P7 pink, p7 black, p9 pink, p7 black, p13 pink, carrying black yarn along behind work for a further 4 sts.
Row 27: K10 pink, k2 black, k2 pink, k5 black, k10 pink, k6 black, k9 pink, carrying black yarn along behind work for a further 3 sts.
Row 28: P6 pink, p2 black, p2 pink, p6 black, p10 pink, p3 black, p2 pink, p4 black, p9 pink.
Row 29: K9 pink, k4 black, k16 pink, k4 black, k2 pink, k4 black, k5 pink.
Row 30: P4 pink, p6 black, p1 pink, p4 black, p17 pink, p2 black, p10 pink.
Row 31: K14 pink, k3 black, k17 pink, k6 black, k4 pink.
Row 32: P5 pink, p4 black, p2 pink, p2 black, p14 pink, p3 black, p14 pink.
Row 33: K14 pink, k2 black, k14 pink, k4 black, k2 pink, k2 black, k6 pink.

Row 34: P10 pink, p4 black, p30 pink.
Row 35: K31 pink, k2 black, k11 pink.
Cut black yarn and weave end in as you
  knit. (Rest of work is in pink.)
Row 36: Purl.
Row 37: Knit.
Row 38: Purl.
Row 39: Knit.
Row 40: Purl.
Row 41: (K2tog, k3) twice, k2, (k2tog, k3)
  four times, k2, (k2tog, k3) twice. 36 sts
Row 42: Purl.
Row 43: (K2tog, k2) twice, k2, kK2tog,
  k2) four times, k2, (k2tog, k2) twice.
  28 sts
Row 44: Purl.
Row 45: (K2tog, k1) twice, k2, (k2tog, k1)
  four times, k2, (k2tog, k1) twice. 20 sts
Row 46: Purl.
Row 47: (K2tog) twice, k2, (K2tog) four
  times, k2, (k2tog) twice. 12 sts
Row 48: Purl.
Row 49: (K2tog) six times. 6 sts
  Cut yarn, leaving a long tail for sewing.
Thread yarn through rem 6 sts and pull
tight. Fasten off, then sew seam using
mattress stitch, leaving gap at the end
for stuffing. Stuff firmly, then sew up
remaining gap. Weave in ends.

Head
Using pink yarn, cast on 12 sts.
Row 1: Knit.

Row 2: Purl.
Row 3: Kfb, k3, kfb, k2, kfb, k3, kfb. 16 sts
Row 4: Purl.
Row 5: Knit.
Row 6: Purl.
Row 7: Kfb, k5, kfb, k2, kfb, k5, kfb. 20 sts
Row 8: Purl.
Row 9: Kfb, k7, kfb, k2, kfb, k7, kfb. 24 sts
Row 10: Purl.
Row 11: Kfb, k8, (kfb) twice, k2, (kfb)
  twice, k8, kfb. 30 sts
Row 12: Purl.
Row 13: Kfb, k11, kfb, k4, kfb, k11, kfb.
  34 sts
Row 14: Purl.
Row 15: Kfb, k13, kfb, k4, kfb, k13, kfb.
  38 sts
Row 16: Purl.
Row 17: Kfb, k15, kfb, k4, kfb, k15, kfb.
  42 sts
Rows 18–24: Beg with a P
row, work 7 rows

in st st.
Row 25: (K2tog, k2) to last 2 sts, k2tog.
  31 sts
Row 26: Purl.
Row 27: (K2tog, k2) to last 3 sts, k2tog,
  k1. 21 sts
Row 28: Purl.
Row 29: (K2tog, k2) to last 3 st, k2tog,
  k1. 17 sts
Row 30: Purl.
Row 31: (K2tog) four times, k1, (k2tog)
  four times. 9 sts
Row 32: Purl.
Cut yarn, leaving a long tail for sewing.
Thread yarn through rem 9
sts, pull tight and fasten
off. Sew seam using

mattress stitch, leaving cast-on edge open. With seam at the bottom of head, place eyes
– it's a bit fiddly through the snout hole, but you should be able to do it. Stuff firmly, shaping as you do so, leaving snout hole open.

Snout

The snout is worked in garter stitch (all knit).
Using pink yarn, cast on 2 sts.
Row 1: Knit.
Row 2: (Kfb) twice. 4 sts
Row 3: Knit.
Row 4: Kfb, k2, kfb. 6 sts
Rows 5–7: Knit.
Row 8: K2tog, k2, k2tog. 4 sts
Row 9: Knit.
Row 10: (K2tog) twice.
Cast off, leaving a long tail for sewing. Sew snout into snout hole, using blanket stitch on the outside to form a ridge around snout. Embroider two nostrils using black yarn.

Ears – make 2, one in black and one in pink

Cast on 11 sts, leaving a long yarn tail.
Rows 1–6: Beg with a K row, work 6 rows in st st.
Row 7: K2tog, k7, k2tog. 9 sts
Row 8: Purl.

Row 9: K2tog, k5, k2tog. 7 sts
Row 10: Purl.
Row 11: K2tog, k3, k2tog. 5 sts
Row 12: Purl.
Row 13: K2tog, k1, k2tog. 3 sts
Row 14: Purl.
Row 15: K3tog and fasten off, leaving a 20cm yarn tail.
Using cast-on yarn tail, sew ears in place in a 'C' shape to make a natural curve. Fasten off. Using remaining yarn, blanket stitch up side of ear to make a neat edge and weave in end. Using cast-off yarn tail, blanket stitch down other side of ear to make a neat edge. Fasten off and weave in end. Fold the ear forward towards snout in a natural shape and fix with a couple of hidden stitches.

Legs – make 4

You can be creative and add black spots to the legs if you wish, but these instructions are for a plain pink leg.
Cast on 4 sts, leaving a 20cm yarn tail for sewing.
Row 1: (Kfb) four times. 8 sts
Row 2: Purl.
Row 3: (Kfb) eight times. 16 sts
Rows 4–10: Beg with a P row, work 7 rows in st st.
Row 11: Kfb, k6, k2tog, k6, kfb. 17 sts
Row 12: Purl.

Row 13: Kfb, k6, k2tog, k7, kfb. 18 sts
Row 14: Purl.
Row 15: Kfb, k6, sk2po, k7, kfb. 18 sts
Row 16: Purl.
Row 17: Knit.
Row 18: Purl.
Row 19: Kfb, k6, kfb, k2, kfb, k6, kfb. 22 sts
Row 20: Purl.
Row 21: Kfb, k8, kfb, k2, kfb, k8, kfb. 26 sts
Rows 22–26: Beg with a P row, work 5 rows in st st.
Row 27: K2tog, k8, k2tog, k2, k2tog, k8, k2tog. 22 sts
Row 28: Purl.
Row 29: K2tog, k6, k2tog, k2, k2tog, k6, k2tog. 18 sts
Row 30: P2tog, p14, p2tog. 16 sts
Cast off, 2tog at each end.
Sew seam from the foot upwards, using cast-on tail end and leaving cast-off stitches open. Stuff leg firmly, then sew gap closed. Weave in ends.

Making up the pig

Cut 40cm pink yarn, thread it through a tapestry needle, then knot both ends of the yarn together to form a loop. Stitch through the body of the pig at the front where the legs will be, and then back again through the body, catching a couple of stiches as you do so. Take the needle through the knotted loop, pull tight to create dimples at either side of the body and fasten off – but do not cut the yarn! Take the needle through one leg at the top, 1cm from the top and side edges, then back again, catching a couple of stitches as you do so, then take the needle back through the dimples in the body and through the top of the second leg, as with the first. Finally, take the needle back through the second leg, through the body, and through the first leg at the same point as before. Pull the yarn tight to make a firm joint for both legs and fasten securely. Weave in ends.

Repeat for the back legs through the pig's rear end.

Sew the raised halves of the snap fasteners to the pig's belly as nipples. Retain the other halves of the fasteners for the piglets.

Tail

Using pink yarn, on dpns cast on 4 sts.

Knit a 5cm Icord. Cut the yarn, leaving a 15cm tail for sewing. Thread the yarn through the stitches and pull tight. Fasten off, then thread the yarn through the length of the tail and pull gently to form a curl. Sew the cast-on end of the tail to the pig's bottom. Weave in ends.

Barbara always enjoyed cuddling Jim's little porker

PIGLETS

Cute baby piggies — make
six of them with different
colour combinations.

Head and body

Using pink yarn, cast on 9 sts, leaving a
15cm yarn tail. Divide the sts evenly over
3 dpns and join to work in the round.
Rounds 1–5: Knit.
Round 6: (K1, kfb, k1) three times. 12 sts
Round 7: K4, kfb, k2, kfb, k4. 14 sts
Round 8: Knit.
Round 9: (Kfb) twice, k10, (kfb) twice. 18 sts
Rounds 10–29: Knit.
Round 30: (K2tog, k1) six times. 12 sts
Round 31: Knit.
Round 32: (K2tog) six times. 6 sts
  Cut yarn, leaving a tail for sewing,
and thread through remaining 6 sts; do
not gather.

Using cast-on yarn tail, thread through
the 6 sts, pull tight, fasten off and weave
in end. Attach eyes above snout. If this
is too difficult, you can embroider eyes
instead with black yarn.
  Stuff piglet firmly, shaping snout
carefully. Pull yarn tight through the 6
stitches and fasten off. Weave in ends.
  Sew flat half of a snap fastener to end of
the piglet's snout with pink thread.

Ears – make 2

Using pink yarn, cast on 7 sts.
Rows 1–7: Beg with a P row, work 7 rows
  in st st.
Row 8: K2tog, k3, k2tog. 5 sts
Row 9: Purl.
Row 10: Knit.
Row 11: Purl.
Row 12: K2tog, k1, k2tog. 3 sts
Row 13: Purl.
Row 14: K3tog and fasten off.
Sew the ears to the piglet's head in the
  same way as for the mother pig.

Legs – make 4

Using pink yarn, cast on 4 sts, leaving a
  20cm yarn tail for sewing.
Row 1: (Kfb) 4 times. 8 sts
Rows 2–6: Beg with a P row, work 5 rows
  in st st.
Row 7: Kfb, k2, (kfb) twice, k2, kfb. 12 sts
Rows 8–10: Beg with a P row, work 3

rows in st st.
Cast off, k2tog at each end.
Sew seam from foot upwards, leaving
cast-off edge open. Stuff legs and sew the
gap shut. Sew legs to piglet's body in the
same way as for the mother pig.

Tail

Using pink yarn, on dpns, cast on 3 sts.
  Knit a 3cm Icord and finish off as for the
mother pig.
  Attach piglets to mum!

POO

Mind you don't step in the ...
oh, too late.

Cast on 5 sts on dpns.
  Knit a 6cm Icord.
  Cut yarn, leaving a 20cm tail for
sewing. Thread yarn through the 5 sts,
pull tight and fasten off, then coil Icord
into a poo shape and sew in place.

Chicken and Egg

One of Jim's rare breed Dans Le Buff chickens. Make yourself a whole coop full!

Skill level
Hard

Finished size
The chicken is 9cm tall.

Materials
* Pair of 2.75mm knitting needles
* Set of four 2.75mm double-pointed knitting needles
* DK yarn in colour of choice – brown, rust, tweed, etc. – for the chicken
* Yellow DK yarn for beak, small amount
* Rusty red DK yarn for cockscomb, small amount
* White baby yarn for egg, small amount
* 2 x 6mm brown safety eyes
* Kapok stuffing
* Thin wire
* 3 small (1cm or smaller) buttons to match main yarn colour
* 3mm crochet hook
* All-purpose glue

CHICKEN

Head
Using yellow yarn, cast on 2 sts, leaving a 10cm yarn tail for sewing.
Row 1: Kfb, k1. 3 sts
Row 2: Purl.
Row 3: K1, (M1, k1) twice. 5 sts
Row 4: Purl.
Row 5: Knit.
Row 6: Purl.
Change to main colour, cutting yellow yarn.
Row 7: K1, (M1, k1) four times. 9 sts
Row 8: Purl.
Row 9: K2, M1, (k1, M1) five times, k2. 15 sts
Row 10: P1, M1, p to last st, M1, p1. 17 sts
Row 11: K1, M1, k14, turn. P13, turn. K11, turn. P9, turn. K7, turn. P5, turn. K10, M1, k1. 19 sts
Row 12: P1, M1, p to last st, M1, p1. 21 sts
Row 13: K1, M1, k1, (ssk) four times, k1, (k2tog) four times, k1, M1, k1. 15 sts
Row 14: P11, turn. K7, turn. P6, turn. K5, turn. Purl.

Cast off, leaving a 20cm tail of yarn for sewing.
Using yellow yarn tail, sew beak seam. Attach eyes on either side of head, close to edge of beak. Using brown yarn tail, sew seam from cast-off edge to beak and carry tyarn back to cast-off edge through back of work. Stuff the head (but not the beak) carefully, shaping as you go. Thread brown yarn tail through cast-off sts and pull closed. Fasten off and weave in any ends.

Body
Using main colour, cast on 4 sts.
Row 1 (Kfb) four times. 8 sts
Row 2: Purl.
Row 3: (Kfb) eight times. 16 sts

43

Row 4: Purl.

Row 5: K1, M1, k6, M1, k2, M1, k6, M1, k1. 20 sts

Row 6: Purl.

Row 7: K1, M1, k7, M1, k4, M1, k7, M1, k1. 24 sts

Row 8: Purl.

Row 9: K1, M1, k13, turn. P4, turn. K5, turn. P6, turn. K7, turn. P8, turn. K to last st, M1, K1. 26 sts

Row 10: Purl.

Row 11: K1, M1, k10, M1, k4, M1, k10, M1, k1. 30 sts

Row 12: Purl.

Row 13: K1, M1, k12, M1, k4, M1, k12, M1, k1. 34 sts

Row 14: Purl.

Row 15: K1, M1, k to last st, M1, k1. 36 sts

Row 16: Purl.

Row 17: K1, M1, k to last st, M1, k1. 38 sts

Row 18: Purl.

Row 19: K1, M1, k13, ssk, k6, k2tog, k13, M1, k1. 38 sts

Row 20: Purl.

Row 21: K1, M1, k13, ssk, k6, k2tog, k13, M1, k1. 38 sts

Row 22: Purl.

Row 23: K1, M1, k3, ssk, k6, k2tog, k1, turn. P10, turn. Ssk, k6, k2tog, k1, turn. P10, turn. Ssk, k6, k2tog, k to last st, M1, k1.** 34 sts

Row 24: P20, turn, k6 – these 6 sts form egg flap.

Row 25: On these 6 sts work 9 rows stst and cast off, leaving long tail for sewing.

Row 26 Rejoin yarn to work and P to end of row.

Row 27: K1, M1, k10, k2tog, k1. 14 sts

Continue working on these 14 sts, leaving the other stitches on the needle (or on a stitch holder if that is easier for you).

Row 28: Purl.

Row 29: K1, M1, k10, k2tog, k1. 14 sts

Row 30: Purl.

Row 31: K1, M1, k8, (k2tog) twice, k1. 13 sts

Row 32: Purl.

Row 33: K1, M1, k7, (k2tog) twice, k1. 12 sts

Cast off.

Rejoin yarn to remaining sts and K1, ssk, k10, M1, k1. 14 sts

Row 34: Purl.

Row 35: K1, ssk, k10, M1, k1. 14 sts

Row 36: Purl.

Row 37: K1, (ssk) twice, k8, M1, k1. 13 sts

Row 38: Purl.

Row 39: K1, (ssk) twice, k7, M1, k1. 12 sts

Cast off, leaving a long tail for sewing.

With right sides together, sew up from egg hole to tip tail and over, then up to neck.

Fasten off and weave in end. Turn right side out.

On dpns, pick up 7 sts from tail end of egg hole to base of flap (needle 1), 6 sts along INNER base of flap (needle 2), then 7 sts from flap to tail (needle 3). Join to work in the round. 20 sts

Work 7 rounds in st st.

Next round: (K1, k2tog) six times, k2tog. 13 sts

Cut yarn, leaving a long tail for sewing. Thread yarn through all 13 sts – do not gather yet. Stuff the body carefully, leaving a gap in the stuffing into which to push the egg pouch. Gather thread in the 13 sts tightly and fasten off. Pass needle through body, out through neck and then through base of head, back through body and out in egg pouch at same spot you entered. Pull tight enough to secure head firmly and hold egg pouch within the body. Fasten off within egg pouch and weave in end.

Using yarn tail on egg flap, pass yarn through work to base of flap and blanket stitch all around the three sides of the flap. Make a buttonhole with the yarn at the top edge of the flap – work two 1cm stitches and blanket stitch along these two stitches together. Fasten off and weave in end. Sew button to chicken's bottom to match with buttonhole.

Collar ruff

Using main colour, cast on 18 sts, leaving
  a long tail for sewing.
Row 1: Purl.
Row 2: K1, kfb, (K3, kfb) four times. 23 sts
Row 3: Purl.
Row 4: K1, M1, (k3, M1) seven times,
  k1. 31 sts
Row 5: Purl.
  Row 6: *Cast on 2 sts, cast off 4 sts, pass
stitch over to left needle*. Repeat from *
to * to end, leaving tail for sewing.
  Using cast-on yarn tail, sew ruff to head,
starting and finishing under the beak and
sewing the seam from top to bottom.
Fasten off and weave in end.
  Using cast-off yarn tail, sew small
running stitches through base of ruff just
above the picots made by casting off,
and pull gently until ruff fits snugly around
the neck. Fasten off and weave in end.
The ruff should hide the neck joint but
allow for movement of the head.

Cockscomb

Using rusty red yarn and crochet hook
chain 20 and leave a long tail for sewing.
Fold chain into 3 consecutive loops (up
and down like an 'M'). Using the yarn
tail, sew through the base of the loops to
hold the loops together. Sew in place on
chicken's head from above the beak to
the back of the head.

Wattles

Using rusty red yarn and crochet hook
chain 25, leaving a tail at either end
for sewing. Using one yarn tail and a
tapestry needle, carefully pull chain
through the head under the beak until
you have two equal lengths. Double
each length into a loop and sew in place
at the point where chain exits the head.
Do not cut the yarn – pass it up through
the head and embroider a red circle
around each eye. Fasten off and weave
in ends.

Wings – make 2

Using main colour, cast on 1 st.
Row 1: Kfbf. 3 sts
Row 2: Purl.
Row 3: K1, M1R, k1, M1L, k1. 5 sts
Row 4: K1, p3, k1.
Row 5: K2, M1R, k1, M1L, k2. 7 sts
Row 6: K1, p5, k1.
Row 7: K3, M1R, k1, M1L, k3. 9 sts
Row 8: K1, p7, k1.
Row 9: K4, M1R, k1, M1L, k4. 11 sts
Row 10: K1, p9, k1.
Row 11: K5, M1R, k1, M1L, k5. 13 sts
Row 12: K1, p11, k1.
Row 13: Knit.
Row 14: K1, p11, k1.
Row 15: Knit.
Row 16: K1, p11, k1.
Row 17: K5, sk2po, k5. 11 sts

Row 18: K1, p9, k1.
Row 19: K4, sk2po, k4. 9 sts
Row 20: K1, k7, k1.
Row 21: K3, sk2po, k3. 7 sts
Row 22: K1, p5, k1.
Row 23: K2, sk2po, k2. 5 sts
Row 24: K1, p3, k1.
Row 25: K1, sk2po, k1. 3 sts
Row 26: Purl.
Row 27: K3tog and keep loop
  open for crochet edging.
Crochet picot edge (ch 3, ss, ch 3
all along edge) on bottom of each
wing, being careful to allow for the fact
they will be on opposite sides of the
chicken! Fasten off and weave in ends.

Sew wings to body

Cut 40cm of main yarn, thread onto
tapestry needle and knot ends of yarn
together to form a loop. Hold one
wing to the side of the chicken to check
placement and pass the needle through
the body at the point where the wing will
attach. Catch a couple of stitches, then
pass the needle back through the body,
out through the first hole and through
the loop of yarn. Pull until there are
two dimples – one on each side of the
chicken's chest – and catch a couple of
stitches to secure. Pass the needle through
the wing, keeping the picot edge at the
bottom. Pass the needle through one

hole in the button and back through the second buttonhole, then back through the wing in the same place, through the body and out through the dimple on the other side. Pass the needle through the second wing and button in the same fashion, then back through the wing, body and first wing. Pull until the wings are securely in place, then fasten under the button to hide the stitching and weave in end.

Legs

This is tricky and needs care.

Cut 30cm of wire and shape one end into a leg, as in the diagram. Thread the straight section through the belly of the chicken in the correct place, going through some of the stuffing as well in order to make the legs more secure, and shape the other end of the straight section in the same way as the first to form the second leg, leaving 2cm of wire at the top of the second leg. Cut off any excess, then poke the 2cm spare wire back through the belly of the chicken to hide it.

Using yellow yarn, start at the top of the leg (you may wish to put a couple of stitches where the wire comes out of the belly in order to secure the yarn while you work), then wind the yarn tightly down the leg to the foot. Wind yarn around the foot and toes, leaving the ends of the toes bare to form the nails. It

might help to place some spots of glue to hold the yarn around the toes. Then wind the yarn back up the leg to the top and around the thigh a few more times to add thickness and shape. Place a spot of glue to keep the end in place and with a tapestry needle, pass the yarn through the thigh a couple of times to secure and weave in end. Repeat for the other leg. Bend the legs into a natural shape so that the chicken can balance to stand.

EGG

Which came first?

Using white baby yarn, cast on 4 sts.
Row 1: (Kfb) four times. 8 sts
Row 2: (Kfb, p1) four times. 12 sts
Row 3: (Kfb, k2) four times. 16 sts
Rows 4–10: Beg with a P row, work 7 rows in st st.
Row 11: (K2tog) eight times. 8 sts
Row 12: (K2tog) four times. 4 sts

Cut yarn, thread through remaining 4 sts and pull tight. Fasten off, then sew seam to almost the end. Stuff firmly, shaping as you do so, then sew rest of seam. Fasten off and weave in ends.

Hide the egg in the chicken's pouch and button up!

Cockerel

Jim's impressive cock – he's always up first thing!

Skill level
Hard

Finished size
The cockerel is 12cm tall.

Materials

* Pair of 2.75mm knitting needles
* Set of four 2.75mm double-pointed knitting needles (dpns)
* Main colour – dark blue, tweedy DK yarn if possible
* Yellow, red, dark blues, greens, teal and black DK yarn, small amounts
* 2 x 6mm brown safety eyes
* Kapok stuffing
* Thin wire
* 2 small (1cm or smaller) buttons to match main yarn colour
* 3mm crochet hook
* All-purpose glue

Head

Using yellow yarn, cast on 2 sts, leaving a
  10cm yarn tail for sewing.
Row 1: Kfb, k1. 3 sts
Row 2: Purl.
Row 3: K1, (M1, k1) twice. 5 sts
Row 4: Purl.
Row 5: Knit.
Row 6: Purl.
Change to red yarn, cutting yellow yarn.
Row 7: K1, (M1, k1) four times. 9 sts
Row 8: Purl.
Row 9: K2, M1, (k1, M1) five times, k2.
  15 sts
Row 10: P1, M1, p to last st, M1, p1. 17 sts
Row 11: K1, M1, k14, turn. P13, turn.
  K11, turn. P9, turn. K7, turn. P5, turn.
  K10, M1, k1. 19 sts
Row 12: P1, MI, p to last st, M1, p1. 21 sts
Row 13: K1, M1, k1, (ssk) four times, k1,
  (k2tog) four times, k1, M1, k1. 15 sts
Row 14: P11, turn. K7, turn. P6, turn. K5,
  turn. Purl.
Cast off, leaving a 20cm tail of yarn for
  sewing.
Using yellow yarn tail, sew beak seam.
Attach eyes on either side of head, close
to edge of beak. Using red yarn tail, sew
seam from cast-off edge to beak and carry
yarn back to cast-off edge through back
of work. Stuff head (but not the beak)
carefully, shaping as you go. Thread yarn
tail through cast-off stitches and pull
closed. Fasten off and weave in any ends.

Body

Using main colour, cast on 4 sts.
Row 1 (Kfb) four times. 8 sts
Row 2: Purl.
Row 3: (Kfb) eight times. 16 sts
Row 4: Purl.
Row 5: K1, M1, k6, M1, k2, M1, k6, M1,
  k1. 20 sts
Row 6: Purl.
Row 7: K1, M1, k7, M1, k4, M1, k7, M1,
  k1. 24 sts
Row 8: Purl.
Row 9: K1, M1, k13, turn. P4, turn. K5,
  turn. P6, turn. K7, turn. P8, turn. K to last
  st, M1, k1. 26 sts
Row 10: Purl.
Row 11: K1, M1, k10, M1, k4, M1, k10,
  M1, k1. 30 sts
Row 12: Purl.
Row 13: K1, M1, k12, M1, k4, M1, k12,
  M1, k1. 34 sts
Row 14: Purl.
Row 15: K1, M1, k to last st, M1, k1. 36 sts
Row 16: Purl.
Row 17: K1, M1, k to last st, M1, k1. 38 sts
Row 18: Purl.
Row 19: K1, M1, k13, ssk, k6, k2tog, k13,
  M1, k1. 38 sts
Row 20: Purl.
Row 21: K1, M1, k13, ssk, k6, k2tog, k13,
  M1, k1. 38 sts
Row 22: Purl.
Row 23: K1, M1, k13, ssk, k6, k2tog, k1,

turn. P10, turn. Ssk, k6, k2tog, k1, turn.
P10, turn. Ssk, k6, k2tog, k to last st, M1,
k1. 34 sts **
Row 24: Purl.
Row 25: K1, M1, k11, ssk, k6, k2tog, k11,
  M1, k1. 34 sts
Row 26: Purl.
Row 27: K1, M1, k9, (ssk) twice, k6, k2tog
  (twice), k9, M1, k1. 32 sts
Row 28: Purl.
Row 29: K1, M1, k8, (ssk) twice, k6,
  (k2tog) twice, k8, M1, k1. 30 sts
Row 30: Purl.
Row 31: K1, M1, k7, (ssk) twice, k6,

(k2tog) twice, k7, M1, k1. 28 sts
Row 32: Purl.
Row 33: K1, M1, k6, (ssk) twice, k6, (k2tog) twice, k6, M1, k1. 26 sts
Cast off, leaving a long tail of yarn for sewing.

   With right sides together, aligning edges, fold body in half. Sew seam up and around tail towards neck, leaving a gap for stuffing. Turn right side out. Stuff, taking care not to over-stuff as the cockerel is supposed to be thinner than the chicken. Sew up the gap and weave in ends.

   Attach head in same way as for the chicken, but sewing through to belly of cockerel instead of the egg pouch.

Collar ruff

Using red yarn, cast on 18 sts, leaving a long tail for sewing.
Row 1: Purl.
Row 2: K1, kfb, (K3, kfb) four times. 23 sts
Row 3: Purl.
Row 4: K1, M1, (k3, M1) seven times, k1. 31 sts
Row 5: Purl.
   Row 6: *Cast on 2 sts, cast off 4 sts, pass stitch over to left needle*. Repeat from * to * to end, leaving tail for sewing.
Using cast-on yarn tail, sew ruff to head, starting and finishing under the beak and sewing the seam from top to bottom. Fasten off and weave in end.
   Using cast-off yarn tail, sew small running stitches through base of ruff just above the picots made by casting off, and pull gently until ruff fits snugly around neck. Fasten off and weave in end. The ruff should hide the neck joint but allow for movement of the head.

Cockscomb

Using red yarn and crochet hook chain 25 and leave a long tail for sewing. Using this tail, fold the chain into 3 consecutive loops (up and down like an 'M'). Sew through base of loops to hold loops together. Sew in place on cockerel's head from above beak to back of head.

The cockerel's cockscomb has larger loops than the chicken.

Wattles

Using red yarn and crochet hook chain 25, leaving a tail at either end for sewing. Using one yarn tail and a tapestry needle, carefully pull chain through head under beak until you have two equal lengths. Double each length into a loop and sew in place at the point where chain exits the head. Do not cut yarn – pass it up through head and embroider a red circle around each eye. Fasten off and weave in ends.

Wings – make 2

Using main colour, cast on 1 st.
Row 1: Kfbf. 3 sts
Row 2: Purl.
Row 3: K1, M1R, k1, M1L, k1. 5 sts
Row 4: K1, p3, k1.
Row 5: K2, M1R, k1, M1L, k2. 7 sts
Row 6: K1, p5, k1.
Row 7: K3, M1R, k1, M1L, k3. 8 sts
Row 8: K1, p7, k1.
Row 9: K4, M1R, k1, M1L, k4. 11 sts
Row 10: K1, p9, k1.
Row 11: K5, M1R, k1, M1L, k5. 13 sts
Row 12: K1, p11, k1.
Row 13: Knit.
Row 14: K1, p11, k1.
Row 15: Knit.

Row 16: K1, p11, k1.
Row 17: K5, sk2po, k5. 11 sts
Row 18: K1, p9, k1.
Row 19: K4, sk2po, k4. 9 sts
Row 20: K1, k7, k1.
Row 21: K3, sk2po, k3. 7 sts
Row 22: K1, p5, k1.
Row 23: K2, sk2po, k2. 5 sts
Row 24: K1, p3, k1.
Row 25: K1, sk2po, k1. 3 sts
Row 26: Purl.
Row 27: K3tog and keep loop open for crochet edging.
Crochet picot edge (ch3, ss, ch3 all along edge) on bottom of each wing, being careful to allow for the fact they will be on opposite sides of the cockerel Fasten off and weave in ends.

Sew wings to body

Cut 40cm of main yarn, thread onto tapestry needle and knot ends of yarn together to form a loop. Hold one wing to the side of the cockerel to check placement and pass the needle through the body at the point where the wing will attach. Catch a couple of stitches, then pass the needle back through the body, out through the first hole and through the loop of yarn. Pull until there are two dimples – one on each side of the cockerel's chest – and catch a couple of stitches to secure. Pass the needle through the wing, keeping the picot edge at the bottom. Pass the needle through one hole in the button and back through the second buttonhole, then back through the wing in the same place, through the body and out through the dimple on the other side. Pass the needle through the second wing and button in the same fashion, then back through the wing, body and first wing. Pull until the wings are securely in place, then fasten under the button to hide the stitching and weave in end.

Legs

This is tricky and needs care.

Cut 32cm of wire (the cockerel's legs are longer than the chicken's) and shape one end into a leg, as in the diagram. Thread the straight section through the belly of the cockerel in the correct place, going through some of the stuffing as well in order to make the legs more secure, and shape the other end of the straight section in the same way as the first to form the second leg, leaving 2cm of wire at the top of the second leg shape. Cut off any excess, then poke the 2cm spare wire back through the belly of the cockerel to hide it.

Using black yarn, start at the top of the leg (you may wish to put a couple of stitches where the wire comes out of the belly in order to secure the yarn while you work), then wind the yarn tightly down the leg to the foot. Wind yarn around the foot and toes, leaving the ends of the toes bare to form the nails. It might help to place some spots of glue to hold the yarn around the toes. Then wind the yarn back up the leg to the top and around the thigh a few more times to add thickness and shape. Place a spot of glue to keep the end in place and with tapestry needle also pass the yarn through the thigh a couple of times to secure and weave in end. Repeat for the other leg. Bend the legs into a natural shape so that the cockerel can balance to stand.

Tail feathers

Using your selection of blues, greens and teal yarns, knit as many lengths as you need, 4–6cm in length, as follows:

Cast on in one colour (10, 12, 14 or 16 sts, depending on length of feather required), then cast off in a contrasting colour; vary the combinations to get a good colour contrast once all the feathers are sewn on.

Weave in one end of yarn from each feather and use the other yarn end to sew the feather in place on the cockerel's tail, facing upwards so that they curve downwards naturally. (See photo for guidance.)

First Aid Tent

Dr Stitch runs the First Aid tent although usually he can be found at the Woolly Bush Medical Centre in the village run by the Knitted Health Service. He graduated with honours from the School of Haberdashery and has a particular interest in moth diseases. He is a keen cricket player, enjoys fishkeeping and has quite an impressive collection of model railways including a model of the famous Blowing Billy Engine.

+FIRST AID

Jim had been told to keep it up all afternoon

3
Food and Drink

The vicar couldn't wait to sample Barbara's cherries

Tea Tent

TASTE
A
RED
BUSH

A Taste Of Barbara's Pantry

The villagers are ready to share their wares and have been busy baking, churning, bottling and growing.

Local
Honey

Honey Honey

Honey

54

Jim was displaying his full moon

Jam or honey jar

Ready to pot up? Use
different-coloured
yarns to make honey, jam,
piccalilli or chutney.

Skill level
Semi

Finished size
The jar is 5cm tall.

Materials
* Set of four 2.75mm double-pointed knitting needles (dpns)
* Pair of 2.75mm knitting needles
* 3mm crochet hook
* DK yarn in mid brown for honey, or red or crimson for jam, small amount
* White DK yarn for lid, small amount
* Small piece of card
* Kapok stuffing
* White felt for label
* Black embroidery thread
* Embroidery needle

Jar
Using your chosen colour of yarn for either jam, honey, chutney or piccalilli, cast on 3 sts.

  Round 1: (Kfb) three times. Divide sts evenly between 3 dpns and join to work in the round. 6 sts
Round 2: (Kfb, k1) three times. 9 sts
Round 3: (Kfb, k2) three times. 12 sts
Round 4: (Kfb, k1) six times. 18 sts
Round 5: Knit.
Round 6: Purl.
Round 7: Knit.
Rounds 8–18. Knit.
Round 19: (K2tog, k1) six times. 12 sts
Round 20: (Kfb, k1) six times. 18 sts
Round 21: Purl.
Cast off knitwise and join last cast-off stitch to first cast-off stitch to tidy up edge. Weave in ends.

Lid
Using white yarn, cast on 3 sts.
Row 1: Purl.
Row 2: Kfb, k1, kfb. 5 sts
Row 3: Kfb, p3, kfb. 7 sts
Row 4: Kfb, k5, kfb. 9 sts
Row 5: Purl.
Row 6: Knit.
Row 7: Purl.
Row 8: K2tog, k5, k2tog. 7 sts
Row 9: P2tog, p3, p2tog. 5 sts
Cast off, k2tog at each end. Transfer last

st to crochet hook.

Crochet row 1: Ch 2, dc 15 all around edge, spacing evenly. SS into 2nd ch.

Crochet row 2: Ch 3, ss into next dc and repeat all round to create picot edging. Cut yarn, leaving a 20cm tail for sewing, and pull through last loop to fasten off.

Making up the jar

Cut two card circles, just big enough to fit inside base of the jar. Place one card circle in base, then stuff with kapok up as far as indented row. Place other card circle on top of stuffing, just below indented row. Add a little more stuffing before attaching the lid.

Fit lid over top of jar and carefully sew all around to lip of jar, leaving crochet edge overhanging the side.

Cut a 20cm length of DK yarn for the 'ribbon'. Thread through the picot edge holes, draw fairly tight and tie a small bow. Trim ends of yarn to tidy.

Label

Using one strand of black embroidery thread, embroider the name of your jam or honey within a 1 x 2cm rectangle of white felt. It is easier to do this before you cut out the label. Cut out the rectangle and sew it to the side of the jar with black embroidery thread, working tiny running stitches to make a border at the same time.

The vicar always enjoyed a cream filling

Battenburg slice

The chequerboard classic!

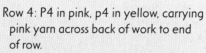

Skill level
Semi

Finished size
The cake is 3.5cm wide.

Materials
* Pair of 2.75mm knitting needles
* DK yarn in pastel yellow, pink and marzipan yellow, small amounts
* Kapok stuffing
* Tapestry needle

First side
As you change colours along the rows, twist the yarns once around each other to prevent making a hole.
Using pastel yellow yarn, cast on 8 sts.
Row 1: K4 in yellow, join pink yarn, k4 in pink.
Row 2: P4 in pink, p4 in yellow.
Row 3: K4 in yellow, k4 in pink.

Row 4: P4 in pink, p4 in yellow, carrying pink yarn across back of work to end of row.
Row 5: K4 in pink, carrying yellow yarn across back of work, k4 in yellow.
Row 6: P4 in yellow, p4 in pink.
Row 7: K4 in pink, k4 in yellow.
Row 8: P4 in yellow, p4 in pink.
Cut yellow yarn and cast off in pink, weaving in yellow yarn end as you go.

Second side
Using pink yarn, cast on 8 sts.
Row 1: K4 in pink, join yellow yarn, k4 in yellow.
Row 2: P4 in yellow, p4 in pink.
Row 3: K4 in pink, k4 in yellow.
Row 4: P4 in yellow, k4 in pink, carrying yellow yarn across to end as before.
Row 5: K4 in yellow, carrying pink yarn across behind work as before, k4 in pink.
Row 6: P4 in pink, p4 in yellow.

Row 7: K4 in yellow, k4 in pink.
Row 8: P4 in pink, p4 in yellow.
Cut pink yarn and cast off in yellow, weaving in pink yarn end as you go.

Marzipan
Using marzipan yellow yarn, cast on 32 sts.
Row 1: Purl.
Row 2: Knit.
Row 3: Purl.
Cast off, leaving a long yarn tail for sewing.

Making up the battenburg slice
Sew two short ends of marzipan together, right sides facing, to form a ring.

With right sides together, sew cast-on edge of marzipan ring around first side of cake, making sure it is evenly spaced and fits the corners correctly.

Repeat with second side of cake and cast-off edge of marzipan ring, making sure you align coloured squares of the two pieces so that they match, and leaving a small gap for turning.

Turn right side out and stuff lightly in order to keep the flat square shape. Sew up the gap.

Using marzipan-coloured yarn, work a few stitches back and forth in each corner to sharpen the edges and shape cake into a square.

Strawberry tart

A juicy strawberry on
soft cream in a pink
cup – perfect!

Skill level
Soft

Finished size
The tart is 4cm in diameter.

Materials

* Set of four 2.75mm double-pointed
  needles (dpns)
* Pink DK yarn, small amount
* Sirdar Snuggly DK yarn in white,
  small amount
* Strawberry red DK yarn, small amount
* Green DK yarn, small amount
* Tapestry needle
* White sewing thread
* Embroidery needle
* Yellow embroidery thread

Base

Using pink yarn, cast on 3 sts.
Round 1: (Kfb) three times. Divide sts
  evenly between 3 dpns and join to work
in the round. 6 sts
Round 2: (Kfb, k1) three times. 9 sts
Round 3: (Kfb, k2) three times. 12 sts
Round 4: (Kfb, k3) three times. 15 sts
Round 5: Knit.
Round 6: Purl.
Round 7: (Kfb, k2) five times. 20 sts
Round 8: Knit.
Round 9: (Kfb, k3) five times. 25 sts
Rounds 10–11: Knit.
Round 12: Purl.
Rounds 13–14: Knit.
Round 15: (K2tog, k3) five times. 20 sts.
Round 16: Knit.
Round 17: (K2tog, k2) five times. 15 sts
Cast off, leaving a long yarn tail for
  sewing.
Join last cast-off stitch to first cast-off stitch
to tidy up edge. Fold work over at second
raised purl round, aligning cast-off edge
with edge of base on the inside. Sew
cast-off edge to edge of base, using
bottom raised purl round as a guide.
Weave in ends.

Cream filling

Using white DK yarn, loosely cast on 30
sts. Loosely cast off all stitches. Cut yarn
ends short. Roll the work into a spiral
and sew together using white sewing
thread, then sew in place inside the tart
base through the inner layer of knitting in
order to hide the stitching.

Strawberry

Using strawberry red yarn, cast on 2 sts.
Row 1: (Kfb) twice. 4 sts
Row 2: (P1, pfb) twice. 6 sts
Row 3: Knit.
Row 4: (P2, pfb) twice. 8 sts
  Cut yarn, leaving a long tail for sewing.
Thread yarn end through sts on needle
and pull tight. Fasten with a stitch and
sew up seam with a couple of stitches.
Weave in yarn ends, shaping the
strawberry by pulling each end gently as
you weave them in.
  Using green yarn, stitch four small
straight stitches in a 'star' shape at the top
of the strawberry for leaves.
  Using two strands of yellow embroidery
thread, embroider tiny straight stitches all
over the strawberry for seeds.
  Sew strawberry to centre of cream filling.

The men fancied a quick stiff one

Eating out

What could be better than getting it alfresco!

Barbara loved tucking in to Patrick's sausage

HOT FOOD

Tomato Ketchup

GET A SAUSAGE IN CIDER

ANY MEAT BETWEEN TWO BAPS

Patrick had got his meat out

Sausage in a bap

A pork sausage slipped between two baps – nice!

Skill level
Soft

Finished size
The bap is 4cm wide without sausage.

Materials
* Pair of 2.75mm knitting needles
* Dark brown DK yarn, small amount
* Cream or white DK yarn, small amount
* Light brown DK yarn, small amount
* Red DK yarn, small amount
* Tapestry needle
* Kapok stuffing

Sausage
Using dark brown yarn, cast on 5 sts.
Row 1: (Kfb) five times. 10 sts
Rows 2–14: Beg with a P row, work 13 rows in st st.
Row 3: (K2tog) five times. 5 sts

Cut yarn, leaving a long tail for sewing. Thread yarn through rem sts and pull tight. Fasten off and sew side seam, leaving cast-on stitches open. Stuff lightly and shape. Thread yarn through cast-on stitches and pull tight. Fasten off and weave in ends. Note: if you want a longer sausage just add more rows in the middle of the patttern.

Bap
Inner section
Using cream or white yarn, cast on 4 sts.
Row 1: Purl.
Row 2: Kfb, k2, kfb. 6 sts
Row 3: Pfb, p4, pfb. 8 sts
Row 4: Kfb, k6, kfb. 10 sts
Row 5: Pfb, p8, pfb. 12 sts
Rows 6–9: Beg with a K row, work 4 rows in st st.
Row 10: K2tog, k8, k2tog. 10 sts
Row 11: P2tog, p6, p2tog. 8 sts
Row 12: K2tog, k4, k2tog. 6 sts
Row 13: P2tog, p2, p2tog. 4 sts
Row 14: Knit.
Row 15: Pfb, p2, pfb. 6 sts
Row 16: Kfb, k4, kfb. 8 sts
Row 17: Pfb, p6, pfb. 10 sts
Row 18: Kfb, k8, kfb. 12 sts
Rows 19–22: Beg with a P row, work 4 rows in st st.
Row 23: P2tog, p8, p2tog. 10 sts
Row 24: K2tog, k6, k2tog. 8 sts
Row 25: P2tog, p4, p2tog. 6 sts
Row 26: K2tog, k2, k2tog. 4 sts
Cast off.

Outer section
Using light brown yarn, cast on 4 sts and knit in exactly the same way as the inner section. When casting off, leave a 30cm yarn tail for sewing.

Making up
With right sides together, sew white and light brown sections together, leaving a 1cm gap for stuffing. Turn right side out – this will be fiddly – and stuff each circular section very lightly, leaving narrow middle part unstuffed. Sew up the gap. Fold in half, white part inside, and sew the sausage horizontally into the bap, catching a few stitches through the work from the outer section in order to shape correctly.

Add 'ketchup' by embroidering a few loops of red DK yarn on the upper part of the sausage, where it meets the bap.

Cider bottle

A quick stiff one!

Skill level
Semi

Finished size
The bottle is 6cm tall.

Materials
* Set of four 2.75mm double-pointed knitting needles (dpns)
* Amber DK yarn, small amount
* Kapok stuffing
* Tapestry needle
* Gold crochet cotton
* Yellow felt, small piece
* Green and black embroidery threads
* Fine sewing needle

Bottle
Using amber yarn, cast on 3 sts.
Round 1: (Kfb) three times. Divide stitches evenly between 3 dpns and join to work in the round. 6 sts

Round 2: (Kfb, k1) three times. 9 sts
Round 3: (Kfb, k2) three times. 12 sts
Round 4: (Kfb, k1) six times. 18 sts
Round 5: Purl.
Round 6: Purl.
Rounds 7–21: Knit.
Stuff bottle; do not break yarn.
Round 22: (K2tog, k4) three times. 15 sts
Round 23: (K2tog, k3) three times. 12 sts
Round 24: (K2tog) six times. 6 sts
Rounds 25–30: Knit.
Cast off, leaving a long tail. Using yarn tail, sew last cast-off stitch to first cast-off stitch to tidy up rim of bottle. Carefully poke stuffing into neck of bottle.

Cap
The cap is knitted straight.
Using gold crochet cotton, cast on 8 sts.
Rows 1–3: Knit.
Row 4: (K2tog) four times. 4 sts
Cut yarn, leaving a tail for sewing.
Thread yarn through rem 4 sts and pull tight. Sew seam, and then fit cap to top of bottle and sew in place.

Label
Cut yellow felt as shown in the diagram and embroider as instructed, using one strand each of gold and black embroidery thread. Sew the label to the bottle, using the photo as a guide.

Pinns bottle

A British summer classic.

Skill level
Semi

Finished size
The bottle is 9cm tall.

Materials

* Set of four 2.75mm double-pointed knitting needles (dpns)
* Amber DK yarn, small amount
* White baby yarn, small amount
* Kapok stuffing
* Tapestry needle
* White felt, small piece
* Red, black and gold embroidery threads
* Fine sewing needle

Bottle

Using amber yarn, cast on 3 sts.
Round 1: (Kfb) three times. Divide stitches evenly between 3 dpns and join to work in the round. 6 sts
Round 2: (Kfb, k1) three times. 9 sts
Round 3: (Kfb, k2) three times. 12 sts
Round 4: (Kfb, k1) six times. 18 sts
Round 5: Purl.
Round 6: Purl.
Rounds 7–26: Knit.
Round 27: (K2tog, k1) six times. 12 sts
Stuff bottle; do not break yarn.
Round 28: (K2tog, k2) three times. 9 sts
Round 29: (K2tog, k1) three times. 6 sts
Round 30: Knit.
Round 31: (Kfb, k1) three times. 9 sts
Round 32: Knit.
Round 33: Knit.
Round 34: (K2tog, k1) three times. 6 sts
Round 35: Knit.
Round 36: Knit.
   Cast off, leaving short yarn tail for sewing. Stitch last cast-off stitch to first cast-off stitch to tidy edge and weave in ends. Carefully poke a little stuffing into neck of bottle to pad out the bulbous centre part.
   Using amber yarn, stitch running stitch from base of bottle at edge of purl rows through to top of purl rows all around, pulling gently as you go to flatten base of bottle. Fasten off and weave in end.

Cap

The cap is knitted straight.
Using white baby yarn, cast on 9 sts.
Row 1: Purl.
Row 2: Knit.
Row 3: Purl.
Row 4: Purl.
Row 5: Knit.
Row 6: P1, (p2tog) four times. 5 sts
   Cut yarn, leaving a 10cm tail for sewing. Thread yarn through rem 5 sts and pull tight. Fasten off, then sew seam to ridge made by purl row. Fit cap to bottle top and sew remaining seam, plus a couple of stitches through bottle neck to keep cap in place.
   Using one strand of red embroidery thread, stitch a line of running stitches around cap just under purl row ridge.

Label

   Mark out a 2 x 3cm rectangle of white felt with a small semi-circle bump at the top of the label. Using one strand of black embroidery thread, embroider the label as shown in the diagram and cut out. Using one strand of gold embroidery thread, blanket stitch the label to the bottle.
   Cut a tiny elongated semi-circle of white felt. Using one strand of gold embroidery thread, blanket stitch it at base of bottle neck.

COCONUT SHY

It was Pattie's first time pegging a ring

Bernard had knocked one off

Coconut

Knit yourself a lovely bunch of coconuts!

Skill level	Finished size
Semi	The coconut is 8cm tall.

Materials

* Set of four 2mm double-pointed knitting needles (dpns)
* Mohair yarn in a camel colour, small amount
* Brown DK yarn, small amount
* Kapok stuffing
* Hi-tack glue
* Tapestry needle

To make the coconut

Using two strands of mohair and one of brown DK yarn, cast on 3 sts.

Round 1: (Kfb) three times. Divide stitches evenly between 3 dpns and join to work in the round. 6 sts

Round 2: (Kfb, k1) three times. 9 sts

Round 3: (Kfb, k2) three times. 12 sts

Round 4: (Kfb, k3) three times. 15 sts

Round 5: (Kfb, k4) three times. 18 sts

Round 6: (Kfb, k2) six times. 24 sts

Rounds 7–16: Knit.

Round 17: (K2tog, k2) six times. 18 sts

Round 18: (K2tog, k4) three times. 15 sts

Round 19: (K2tog, k3) three times. 12 sts

Round 20: (K2tog, k3) three times. 9 sts

Stuff the coconut through the hole, break off yarns and thread through remaining 9 sts. Sew the gap closed. Thread a tapestry needle with one strand each of camel and brown yarn. Sew several short lengths (about 5cm) around the cast-off area. Sew several more just below the first set. Gently brush upwards to form a tuft. Coat the tuft with hi-tack glue and allow to dry. Trim with scissors to get the tuft looking perfect!

(pattern by Michelle Green)

69

WOOLLY BUSH
WILDLIFE RESCUE

COME IN
AND STROKE
A WEASEL

HELP US
GET OUR
HANDS ON
MORE TITS

BUMPER
BOOK
OF
TITS

SEE A
BADGER
UP CLOSE

Wildlife Rescue

The fair has a tent run by
Woolly Bush Wildlife Rescue to
encourage visitors to discover
what wildlife could be lurking
in their back garden or passage.
There's the opportunity to get
hands on and up close with some
of the animals, with badgers to
stroke and great tits to admire.

Recently the vicar has been running a campaign to reintroduce beavers into Woolly Bush – The Woolly Bush Beaver Project. Originally just four were let loose in Harden Forest but now beavers can be spotted all over the village. Out with his binoculars, even if he isn't always lucky enough to see one, he knows there is usually a beaver nearby by finding tell-tale beaver wood. As the vicar says, 'If you have wood you know a beaver won't be far away!'

4
Sports

Bernard was pulling back very hard

Sporting Chance
All of a Quiver

A rare chance to draw back hard and hear that unmistakable thwack as it hits the target. Lord and Lady Fairisle open up the grounds of Raglan Hall in the summer for various events and during the Woolly Bush Carnival archery is available for everyone to try. To have your best shot at getting it in the bullseye it's important you have a straight shaft and keep a steady hand.

Bernard just couldn't get it to stay in

Archery set

Bullseye!

Skill level
Hard

Finished size
Target: 28cm tall
Bow: 21cm long
Arrow: 18cm long

Materials

* 3mm crochet hook
* Pair of 3mm knitting needles
* DK yarn in yellow, red, light blue, black, white and light brown, small amounts
* Foamboard, small amount
* Light brown felt, small amount
* White sewing thread
* Sewing needle
* White crochet cotton (30cm only)
* Template (see note on page 95)
* Craft knife or scalpel
* All-purpose glue
* Cocktail sticks

TARGET

Using yellow yarn and magic loop method, work 6 dc, pull loop tight and join with ss into first dc.
Round 1: Ch 1, 2 dc into each dc, ss into ch.
Round 2: Ch 1, (1 dc, 2 dc in next dc) all round, ss into ch.
Round 3: Change to red yarn. Ch 1, (2 dc, 2 dc into next 2 dc) all round, ss into ch.
As the work grows, you may have odd numbers of stitches at the end of each round; just dc into these before ss into the ch – it does not affect the circle you are making.
Round 4: Ch 1, (2 dc, 2 dc into next dc) all round, ss into ch.
Round 5: Ch 1, (3 dc, 2 dc into next dc) all round, ss into ch.
Round 6: Change to light blue yarn. Ch 1, (3 dc, 2 dc into next dc) all round, ss into ch.
Round 7: Ch 1, (4 dc, 2 dc into next dc) all round, ss into ch.
Round 8: Ch 1, (4 dc, 2 dc into next dc) all round, ss into ch.
Round 9: Change to black yarn. Ch 1, (6 dc, 2 dc into next dc) all round, ss into ch.
Round 10: Ch 1, (8 dc, 2 dc into next dc) all round, ss into ch.
Round 11: Ch 1, dc all round, ss into ch.
Round 12: Change to white yarn. Ch 1, dc all round, ss into ch.
Round 13: Ch 1, dc all round, ss into ch.
Round 14: Ch 1, dc all round, ss into ch and fasten off.
Cut a circle of foamboard the same size as your crocheted target.
Cut a circle of light brown felt the same size as your crocheted target.
Place the foamboard in between the felt and crochet and blanket stitch the layers together using white sewing thread.

Target legs

Cut two strips of foamboard 1cm wide and 10cm long.
Cut one strip of foamboard 1cm wide

and 13cm long.

You can either cover the legs by cutting felt to size and sewing it around the foamboard, or you can knit the covering with light brown DK yarn.

To knit the covering

Cast on 10 sts and work in st st to the length required for each leg. Sew the knitting around the foamboard strips, keeping the seam at the centre back.

Assembling the target

Sew the two shorter legs to the back of the target at either side, placing the top level with centre of target and leaving 2cm of leg protruding from the bottom of the target. These legs should be firmly fixed.

Sew the top edge only of the longer leg to the back of the target at the centre in order to create a hinge. Adjust if necessary to ensure that the target stands firm, like an easel.

BOW AND ARROWS

Remember to draw back hard…

Bow

Cut the shape of the bow from foamboard, using the template. You will have to use a scalpel or craft knife to do this, so be very careful not to cut through the thin shape – or yourself!

Glue one end of light brown yarn to the foamboard and wind the yarn carefully around the full length of the bow, covering all the foamboard. Glue the end and trim any excess yarn once the glue is dry.

When the glue is dry, sew one end of the white crochet cotton securely to one tip of the bow, stretch tightly (but not so tight that you bend the bow!) and sew to the other tip of the bow.

Arrows

Trim one end of a cocktail stick, and wind light brown yarn around it in the same way as for the bow. Glue the yarn in place and trim any ends. Make 'flights' by sewing or gluing scraps of red DK yarn in place at the blunt end of the arrow.

For arrowhead, cast on 1 st in light brown.

Round 1: Kfb. 3sts
Round 2: P3.
Round 3: K1, kfb, k1. 4 sts

Cast off P-wise. Fold triangle over head of arrow, cast on stitch as point, sew the small seam at same time as sewing to arrow to secure in place.

A Jolly Good Tug

The tug of war takes place on the village green — everyone grabs hold and starts tugging on PC Bobble's whistle.

As PC Bobble blew everyone got a tight grip

Highland Fling

Jim's father, Jimmy McFurry, is Scudburgh's most decorated Highland Games winner – there's nothing he doesn't know about handling large wood. The games, sponsored by local companies Bunnocks and Ironing Bru are the highlight of the Scottish calendar.

Jimmy has a small holding in Scudburgh where he breeds Tartan Shorthorn cattle. His dog Toorie might look similar to Willie – that's because he is Willie's uncle!

Jim uses the carnival to show the villagers his own talents at the Highland Games – he tosses his caber to great effect and his hammer action is quite outstanding.

Jimmy always excelled at tossing

Jim was used to handling a large wood

Pattern for Jim

Jim, his red and white scarf and Knitter branded wellies!

Skill level
Hard

Finished size
Jim is approx. 30cm tall.

Materials

* Pair of 2.75mm knitting needles
* Sirdar Hayfield Bonus DK in Biscuit 963 for flesh tones
* Stitch holder(s)
* Tapestry needle
* Templates (see note on page 95)
* Craft knife
* 10cm polystyrene ball (preferably egg shaped) for the body
* 7cm polystyrene ball for the head
* A pack of 100 30cm white pipe cleaners
* Sticky tape
* Quilt wadding, small amount
* Toy stuffing
* 2 x 10mm glass eyes in green
* All-purpose glue
* Orange yarn for hair, small amount
* Pink embroidery thread, small amount
* Embroidery needle
* Pink or red colouring pencil

To make Jim

Use the flesh-coloured yarn for all body parts.

Knit in stocking stitch throughout, unless otherwise instructed.

Sole of foot – make 2

Cast on 6 sts.
Row 1: Pfb, p to last st, pfb. 8 sts
Row 2: Kfb, k to last st, kfb. 10 sts
Rows 3–15: Beginning with a P row, work 13 rows in st st.
Row 16: K6, k2tog. 9 sts
Row 17: Purl.
Row 18: K5, k2tog. 8 sts
Row 19: Purl.
Row 20: K2tog, k to end. 7 sts
Row 21: Purl.
Cast off.
Make another sole, reversing all shaping.

Foot upper – make 2

Cast on 6 sts.
Row 1: Knit.
Row 2: Purl.
Row 3: Kfb, k to last st, kfb. 8 sts
Row 4: Purl.
Rows 5–8: Rep rows 3–4 twice. 12 sts
Row 9: Kfb, k4, kfb, k to last st, kfb. 15 sts
Row 10: Purl.
Row 11: K7, kfb, k7. 16 sts
Row 12: Purl.
Row 13: K8, kfb, k8. 17 sts
Row 14: Purl.
Row 15: K8, kfb, k8. 18 sts
Row 16: Purl.
Row 17: K9, kfb, k9. 19 sts
Row 18: Purl.
Row 19: K9, k2tog, k to end. 18 sts
Row 20: Purl.
Row 21: K5, (k2tog) twice, turn work leaving rem 9 sts unworked and cont

working on these 7 sts only.

Row 22: Purl.

Row 23: K to last 2 sts, k2tog. 6 sts

Row 24: Purl.

Row 25: K to last 2 sts, k2tog. 5 sts

Rows 26–30: Beg with a P row, work 5 rows in st st.

Cast off.

With RS facing, rejoin yarn to rem 9 sts, (k2tog) twice, then rep rows 22–30, reversing all shaping. Cast off.

Legs – make 2

Cast on 15 sts.

Rows 1–12: Beg with a K row, work 12 rows in st st.

Row 13: Kfb, k to last st, Kfb. 17 sts

Row 14: Purl.

Rows 15–20: Beg with a K row, work 6 rows in st st.

Row 21: Pfb, k to last st, pfb. 19 sts

Row 22: Purl.

Rows 23–30: Beg with a K row, work 8 rows in st st.

Row 31: Pfb, k to last st, pfb. 21 sts

Row 32: Purl.

Rows 33–44: Beg with a K row, work 12 rows in st st.

Rows 45–50: Beg with a K row, work 6 rows in st st.

Cast off.

Neck – make 1

Cast on 14 sts.

Beg with a P row, work 5 rows in st st.

Cast off.

Nose – make 1

Cast on 6 sts.

Beg with a P row, work 3 rows in st st.

Break yarn, thread through sts, pull up tightly and secure, leaving a long tail.

Ears – make 2 fronts and 2 backs

Front of ear

Cast on 3 sts.

Row 1 (WS): Purl.

Row 2: Kfb, k1, kfb. 5 sts

Row 3: Purl.

Row 4: K to last st, kfb. 6 sts

Row 5: Pfb, purl to end. 7 sts

Row 6: K to last stitch, pfb. 8 sts

Row 7: P2tog, purl to end. 7 sts

Cast off.

Back of ear

Cast on 3 sts.

Row 1 (WS): Purl.

Row 2: Kfb, k to last st, kfb. 5 sts

Row 3: Purl.

Row 4: Kfb, knit to end. 6 sts

Row 5: P to last st, pfb. 7 sts

Row 6: Pfb, k to end. 8 sts

Row 7: P2tog, p to end. 7 sts

Cast off.

Arms – make 2

Note: Nudinits only have 3 fingers and a thumb on each hand.

Cast on 8 sts.

Row 1: Knit.

Row 2: Purl.

Row 3: Kfb, k to last st, kfb. 10 sts

Row 4: Purl.

Rows 5–12: Rep rows 3–4 four

times. 18 sts
Row 13: Purl.
Row 14: K2tog, k to last 2 sts, k2tog. 16 sts
Row 15: Purl.
Rows 16–29: Beg with a K row, work 14 rows in st st.
Row 30: K2tog, k to 2 last sts, k2tog. 14 sts
Row 31: Purl.
Rows 32–35: Beg with a K row, work 4 rows in st st.
Row 36: K2tog, k to 2 last sts, k2tog. 12 sts
Row 37: Purl.
Rows 38–45: Beg with a K row, work 8 rows in st st.
Row 46: K2tog, k to 2 last sts, k2tog. 10 sts
Rows 47–49: Beg with a P row, work 3 rows in st st.
Row 50: (Kfb) ten times. 20 sts
Row 51: Purl.
Row 52: (Kfb) twice, k to last 2 sts, (kfb) twice. 24 sts
Row 53: Purl.
Note: At this point you work separately on the front and back of each finger, working 3 finger fronts, a thumb, then 3 finger backs, so you will have something resembling an octopus when finished!
Row 54: *K3, turn.
Row 55: Purl.
Cont on these 3 sts only and beg with a K row, work 16 rows in st st.
Break yarn, leaving a long tail. Using a tapestry needle, thread yarn through the

3 sts. Take sts off knitting needle, pass tapestry needle back through the 3 sts again and pull tight *.
With RS facing, rejoin yarn and repeat from * to * twice more, making a total of 3 fingers.
With RS facing, rejoin yarn, k6 and turn, leaving remaining sts unworked; this will make the front <u>and</u> back of the thumb.
Next row: Purl.
Beg with a K row, work 12 rows in st st.
K3tog, break off yarn and pull it through the remaining st; this completes one side of the thumb.
Rejoin yarn, k3tog, break off yarn and pull it through the remaining st; this completes the other side of the thumb.
Rejoin yarn to remaining 9 sts and repeat from * to *, making another 3 fingers.

Palm – make 2
Note: The palm is made in garter stitch (all knit).
Cast on 4 sts.
Row 1: Knit
Row 2: Kfb, k to last st, kfb. 6 sts
Rows 3–5: Knit.
Row 6: K2tog, k to last 2 sts, k2tog. 4 sts
Row 7: Knit.
Cast off.

Back of hand – make 2
Cast on 6 sts.

Row 1: Knit.
Row 2: Purl.
Row 3: Kfb, k to last st, kfb. 8 sts
Row 4: Purl.
Rows 5–8: Beg with a K row, work 4 rows in st st.
Row 9: K2tog, k to last 2 sts, k2tog. 6 sts
Row 10: Purl.
Cast off.

Willy – make 1
Note: It is advised not to make this pattern any longer than stated, as it may lead to feelings of insecurity in other nudinits.
Cast on 8 sts.
Rows 1–4: Beg with a K row, work 4 rows in st st.
Row 5: Kfb, k to end. 9 sts
Row 6: Purl.
Rows 7–10: Rep rows 5–6 twice. 11 sts
Rows 11–12: Beg with a K row, work 2 rows in st st.
Cast off.

Head – make 1 back part and 1 front part
Back of head
Cast on 15 sts.
Row 1: Knit.
Row 2: Purl.
Row 3: Kfb, k to last st, kfb. 17 sts
Row 4: Purl.
Rows 5–12: Rep rows 3–4 four times.

25 sts
Rows 13–20: Beg with a K row, work 8
  rows in st st.
Row 21: K2tog, k to last 2 sts, k2tog. 23 sts
Row 22: Purl.
Rows 23–30: Rep rows 21–22 four times.
  15 sts
Row 31: (K2tog) twice, k to last 4 sts,
  (k2tog) twice. 11 sts
Row 32: Purl.
Rows 33–34: Rep rows 31–32. 7 sts
Cast off.

Front of head

Cast on 14 sts.
Row 1: Knit.
Row 2: Purl.
Row 3: Kfb, k to last st, kfb. 16 sts
Row 4: Purl.
Rows 5–20: Rep rows 3–4 eight times.
  32 sts
Rows 21–24: Beg with a K row, work 4
  rows in st st.
Row 25: K2tog, k to last 2 sts, k2tog. 30 sts
Row 26: Purl.
Rows 27–38: Rep rows 25–26 six times.
  18 sts
Row 39: K2tog, k to last 2 sts, k2tog. 16 sts
Row 40: P2tog, p to last 2 sts, p2tog. 14 sts
Rows 41–42: Rep rows 39–40. 10 sts
Cast off.

Body (make one front part and one back part)

Front of body

Cast on 22 sts.
Row 1 (WS): Purl.
Row 2: Kfb, k to last st, kfb. 24 sts
Row 3: Purl.
Rows 4–13: Rep rows 2–3 five times.
  34 sts
Rows 14–21: Beg with a K row, work 8
  rows in st st.
Row 22: K2tog, k to last st, k2tog. 32 sts
Row 23: Purl.
Rows 24–27: Beg with a K row, work 4
  rows in st st.
Row 28: K2tog, k to last 2 sts, k2tog.
  30 sts
Row 29: Purl.
Rows 30–45: Rep rows 28–29 eight
  times. 14 sts
Row 46: Knit.
Row 47: Purl.
Row 48: K2tog, k to last 2 sts, k2tog. 12 sts
Row 49: Purl.
Cast off.

Back of body

Cast on 22 sts.
Row 1n (WS): Purl.
Row 2: Kfb, k to last st, kfb. 24 sts
Row 3: Purl.
Rows 4–13: Rep rows 2–3 five times. 34 sts
Rows 14–21: Beg with a K row, work 8
  rows in st st.
Row 22: K2tog, k to last 2 sts, k2tog. 32 sts
Row 23: Purl.
Rows 24–27: Beg with a K row, work 4
  rows in st st.
Row 28: K2tog, k to last 2 sts, k2tog. 30 sts
Row 29: Purl.
Rows 30–35: Rep rows
  28–29 three times. 24 sts
Row 36: Knit.
Row 37: Purl.
Row 38: K2tog, k to last 2
  sts, k2tog. 22 sts
Row 39: Purl.
Rows 40–49:
  Rep rows
  38–39 five
  times. 12 sts
Cast off.

Making up Jim

For materials, see page 80.
For templates, see page 95.
  Weave in cast-on and
cast-off ends before you start
sewing body parts together.
Use the flesh-coloured yarn
used to knit Jim to sew the
knitted pieces together.

To make the skeleton
For the body
Using the 10cm polystyrene ball, cut a slice off each side to leave a 3cm-thick part in the middle. Keep shaping the edges of the middle part until it resembles the body template. Take the two larger side pieces cut off earlier and shape into two feet shapes to look like the foot template. Make a hole in each foot where indicated.

For the head
Using the 7cm polystyrene ball, cut a slice off each side to leave a 4cm piece in the middle. Shape this until it resembles the head template.

For the arms and hands
Twist 12 pipe cleaners together, holding them against the arm template to get the arm length correct, then separate the remaining length into 4 groups of 3 and twist each of these groups together to make 4 fingers. Using the finger template, cut the fingers to the correct length. Repeat for the second arm.

For the legs
Twist 6 pipe cleaners together. Poke one end of the twist right through a polystyrene foot. Bend 3cm of twisted pipe cleaners over at a right angle and secure with sticky tape under the foot. Repeat for the second leg.

For the neck
Take 1 pipe cleaner and fold it into 4, then twist the folded length together.

Assembling the skeleton
Using the skeleton template as a guide, poke the arms and legs into the polystyrene body. Poke one end of the neck into the body and the other end into the head. Wrap wadding around the body and sew together at the shoulders, crotch and up both sides. Wrap wadding tightly around the legs and sew together. Wrap and sew a little wadding around the upper arms. Cover the head with wadding and sew together around the head, then sew a small piece around the neck.

Note: As you do this, you can put stuffing between the wadding and body, depending on how fat you want Jim to be.

To sew the body
With WS facing, sew back seam on upper foot. Place sole in position and, with WS facing, sew sole to bottom of foot. Repeat for other foot. Turn both feet right side out and pull over the polystyrene feet.

Wrap the knitted leg pieces around each leg skeleton and sew seams. (The seams should run on the inner leg, not at the back.) Stitch the bottom of the leg onto the foot.

Place the front and back knitted body pieces onto the skeleton and sew together along both sides, across the shoulders and under the crotch. As you do this, you can add stuffing to create a bigger belly or buttocks.

Catch down the tops of the knitted legs onto the body.

Sew the head parts over the skeleton head, leaving the neck open. As you go, push in tiny bits of stuffing to give shape to the cheeks, chin and back of the head.

Wrap the neck piece around the skeleton neck and sew the ends together. Then catch the neck piece down onto the body and head edges.

Position the arm pieces over the skeleton arms and sew the long seam, positioning the seam under the armpit.

Sew the finger seams together around the pipe-cleaner fingers — the thumb only has one seam, as it was knitted in one piece instead of two like the fingers.

Catch down the knitted arm edges to the free edges of the body to create shoulder seams.

Squeeze the fingers together at the base. Pull the thumb out slightly. Sew the knitted back of the hand onto the skeleton back of the hand and the knitted palm onto the skeleton palm.

With a long needle and flesh-coloured yarn, secure the yarn at the crotch. Bring the needle up through the stuffing inside the puppet and out at the belly button (use the photo as a guide), then push the needle back in and down towards the crotch, making sure you catch at least one knitted stitch. Bring the needle back out at the crotch and pull on the yarn slightly to create the belly-button indentation. Secure the yarn with a small backstitch, then work a small running stitch up the centre of the buttocks. When you get to where you feel is the top of the buttocks, push the needle back down and pull it out at the crotch. Pull on the yarn slightly to get the buttock shape. Secure the yarn tightly with a small backstitch to hold the shape.

With RS together, sew together 1 knitted ear front and back, leaving the long edge free. Turn right side out. Repeat for the second ear. Sew the ears onto the head, attaching them along the long edge.

Lightly stuff the nose, and with a running stitch pull together the cast-on edge of the nose. Sew the nose onto the face.

Position the eyes on the head, using the photo as a guide, and glue in place. Using flesh-coloured yarn, make a long stitch over the top and bottom of the eye to give the eye shape.

Roll up the willy piece tightly, right side out, and catch together with a few stitches to stop it becoming loose. Sew in position on the body.

Using orange yarn, embroider loose French knots over Jim's face and head as shown to create a full beard and hair at the back of the head, leaving a bald head at the top. Embroider the eyebrows in straight stitch. Use the same French knot technique to create pubic hair and armpit hair.

Using pink embroidery thread, work a mouth in backstitch and nipples in satin stitch.

Using a craft knife, finely scrape red or pink pencil lead onto a piece of paper. Rub your finger in the powder, then rub a little into the cheeks on the face, bottom, knees, elbows and belly button.

JIM'S SCARF

Skill level
Soft

Materials
* Pair of 3mm knitting needles
* Red DK yarn, small amount
* White DK yarn, small amount
* Small snap fastener
* White sewing thread
* Sewing needle

To make scarf
Using red yarn, cast on 1 st.
Row 1: Kfbf. 3 sts
Row 2: Pfb, join white yarn, p1 white, pfb red. 5 sts
Row 3: (Kfb – KF red, KB white), k3 red, (kfb – KF white, KB red). 7 sts
Row 4: Pfb red, p2 red, p1 white, p2 red, pfb red. 9 sts
Row 5: Kfb red, k1 red, k1 white, k3 red, k1 white, k1 red, kfb red. 11 sts
Row 6: Pfb red, p1 white, p3 red, p1 white, p3 red, p1 white, pfb red. 13 sts
Row 7: (Kfb – KF red, KB white), k3 red, k1 white, k3 red, k1 white, k3 red, (kfb – KF white, KB red). 15 sts
Row 8: Pfb red, p2 red, p1 white, p3 red, p1 white, p3 red, p1 white, p2 red, pfb 1 red. 17 sts

Row 9: Kfb red, k1 red, k1 white, k3 red, k1 white, k3 red, k1 white, k3 red, k1 white, k1 red, kfb red. 19 sts
Row 10: Pfb red, p1 white, p3 red, p1 white, p3 red, p1 white, p3 red, p1 white, p3 red, p1 white, pfb red. 21 sts
Row 11: Cast on 5 sts in red, k9 red, k1 white, k3 red, k1 white, k3 red, k1 white, k3 red, k1 white, k3 red, kfb red. Cut white yarn. 27 sts
Row 12: Cast on 5 sts, p to end in red. 32 sts
Cast off and weave in ends.
Using white sewing thread, sew a snap fastener to the ends of the bandana, checking that it fits your puppet.
If you prefer a tie fastening, cast on 5 extra stitches in rows 11 and 12.
You may need to press the scarf with an iron to stop it from curling.

JIM'S WELLIES

Skill level

Soft

Finished size

7.5cm long and 7.5cm tall

Materials

* Pair of 3mm knitting needles
* Sage green DK yarn, small amount
* Tapestry needle
* Template (see note on page 95)
* Black felt, small amount
* Black embroidery thread
* White felt, small amount
* Red embroidery thread
* Embroidery needle

Top section – make 2

Using sage green yarn, cast on 45 sts.
Rows 1–5: Beg with a P row, work 5 rows in st st.
Row 6: K20, ssk, k1, k2tog, k20. 43 sts
Row 7: P19, p2tog, p1, p2tog, p19. 41 sts
Row 8: K18, ssk, k1, k2tog, k18. 39 sts
Row 9: P17, p2tog, p1, p2tog, p17. 37 sts
Row 10: K16, ssk, k1, k2tog, k16. 35 sts
Row 11: P15, p2tog, p1, p2tog, p15. 33 sts
Row 12: K12, (ssk) twice, k1, (k2tog) twice, k12. 29 sts

Row 13: P10, (p2tog) twice, p1, (p2tog) twice, p10. 25 sts
Row 14: Knit.
Row 15: Purl.
Row 16: K1, kfb, k10, kfb, k10, kfb, k1. 28 sts
Row 17: Purl.
Row 18: K1, kfb, k12, M1, k12, kfb, k1. 31 sts
Row 19: Purl.
Row 20: K1, kfb, k13, kfb, k13, kfb, k1. 34 sts
Rows 21–29: Beg with a P row, work 9 rows in st st.
Cast off, leaving a 30cm tail of yarn for sewing.
Fold each welly in half lengthways and sew the back seam using mattress stitch.

Assembling the wellies

Using the template, cut out two sole shapes in black felt. Using blanket stitch and black embroidery thread, blanket stitch the soles to the wellies.

Mark out a 1.5 x 5cm rectangle on white felt. Within the shape, using one strand of black embroidery thread, embroider the word 'Knitter'. Cut out the rectangle and sew it to the top of the boot at the front, using one strand of red embroidery thread and small running stitches.

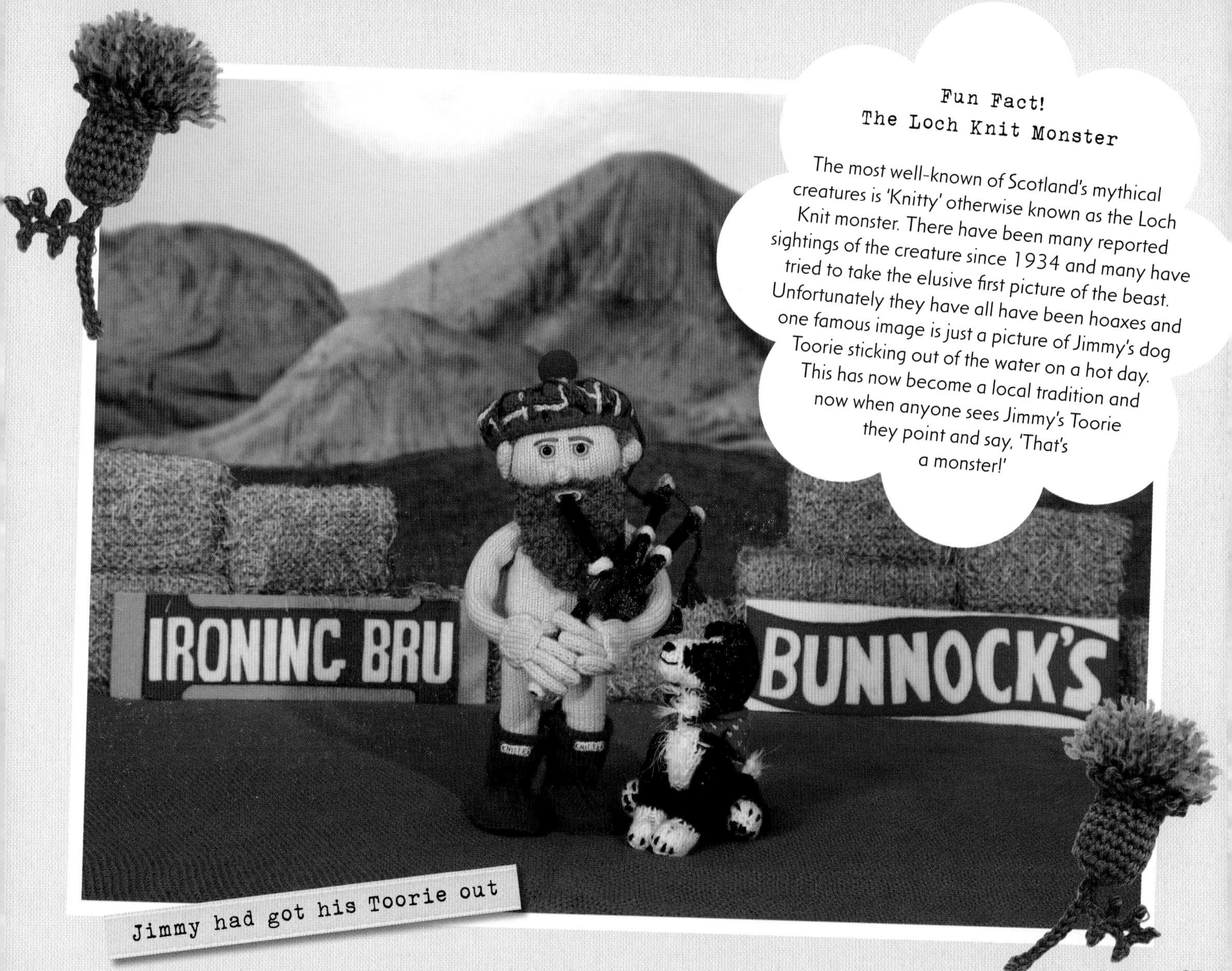

IRONINC BRU
BUNNOCK'S

Jimmy had got his Toorie out

Fun Fact!
The Loch Knit Monster

The most well-known of Scotland's mythical creatures is 'Knitty' otherwise known as the Loch Knit monster. There have been many reported sightings of the creature since 1934 and many have tried to take the elusive first picture of the beast. Unfortunately they have all have been hoaxes and one famous image is just a picture of Jimmy's dog Toorie sticking out of the water on a hot day. This has now become a local tradition and now when anyone sees Jimmy's Toorie they point and say, 'That's a monster!'

PC Bobble blew hard
on his whistle

Cheese Rolling

Held on Bushy Mound, the carnival ends with the tradition of cheese rolling. One of Jim's Full Moon cheeses is tossed off the top of the hill and the villagers then race down to try and catch it. Whoever reaches the bottom first and gets their hands on Jim's Full Moon is the winner!

The chase is on for Jim's full moon!

Nature In Peril Society

HELP US SAVE THE LOCAL WILDLIFE OF WOOLLY BUSH

- Save our endangered satin smooth newts

- Beaver Watch! Tell us how many beavers you've seen over one weekend

- Spend an afternoon twitching with the vicar – he'll show you the difference between a penduline tit and a great tit!

- Help us tidy up Bushy Mound – keep your area clean!

The Woolly Bush Tea Rooms

Afternoon Delight

* Cream on top? It's up to you with **our scones!**

* Get your lips around a **lapson souchong!**

* Fingers and fizz, **afternoon tea** with a difference!

TASTE A RED BUSH

* Find us on **Woolly Bush** High Street

Bunnock's Tea Cakes
A lovely creamy mouthful

STOCKED IN
WOOLTROSE

BUNNOCK'S

GET YOUR HANDS ON A PAIR OF BUNNOCK'S TODAY!

WOOLLY BUSH TAXI SERVICE

'We always know the way and won't come off too soon'

Let us know if you like to come a particular way

We have all sizes and can get anything in the back

Reliable and friendly – call us today on *Woolly Bush 4444*

Bumtree

- Pre-loved organ for sale
- One careful owner
- Only played with on a Sunday
- First to see will take it

Please contact Rev Cecil Felting on Woolly Bush 6969

'One Man and his Willie' TV show

This fantastic series sees sheepdogs and their handlers competing to win first prize on 'One Man and his Willie'

Admire how a professional handles his Willie under pressure

Presented by Ben Ogle with commentary by Anita Fani

'I love to watch Jim being in complete control of his Willie – a must see on a Sunday evening!'
Rev Cecil Felting

Available to watch on Knitflix

ABBREVIATIONS

Ch Chain
DC Double Crochet
DPN(s) Double-pointed needle(s)
K Knit
K2tog Knit 2 stitches together (1 stitch decreased)
K3tog Knit 3 stitches together (2 stitches decreased)
Kbfb Knit into back, front, then back of same stitch (2 stitches increased)
Kfb Knit into front then back of same stitch (1 stitch increased)
Kfbf Knit into front, back, then front of same stitch (2 stitches increased)
M1 Using tip of left needle, pick up horizontal strand of yarn between last stitch on right needle and first stitch on left needle, from front to back, and place it onto left needle, then knit through back loop (1 stitch increased)
M1L Make one left
M1R Make one right

MB Make bobble: knit into front and back of next st, turn, p2, turn, k2tog.
P Purl
P2tog Purl 2 stitches together (1 stitch decreased)
P3tog Purl 3 stitches together (2 stitches decreased)
RS Right side of work
SK2PO Slip 1 stitch, knit 2 stitches together, pass slipped stitch over (2 stitches decreased)
SS Slip stitch
SSK Slip 1 stitch, slip 1 stitch, knit 2 slipped stitches together through back loops (1 stitch decreased)
St St Stocking (stockinette) stitch
WS Wrong side of work

TEMPLATES

For all patterns that require templates, you can find them online at www.nudinits.com or www.pavilionbooks.com.

RECOMMENDED STOCKISTS

For yarn we like www.deramores.com and www.lovecrafts.com
For pipe cleaners, polystyrene balls and other bits and pieces we used www.hobbycraft.com
For the characters eyes we use teddy bear eyes from www.handglasscraft.com This, among other reasons, means that nudinit puppets are not suitable for children

THANK YOU

Thank you to all at Pavilion, Sophie, Frida and Alice especially. I'd also like to thank Ed Hartwell, Caroline Bletsis, Michelle Green, Leeanne Bell, Sally Bentham, Jacqui Hurst and Carol Law for all their contributions to this book. The whole thing was photographed, written, knitted, made, designed and drawn during lockdown so a special and enormous thank you to all those above who kept calm and carried on despite home schooling, shielding, caring, self-isolating and drinking too much (although the last one may have just been me).

CREDITS

All nudinit set photography by Ed Hartwell
All cut out photography by Jacqui Hurst
Character patterns by Sarah Simi
All other patterns by Caroline Bletsis apart from Coconut pattern by Michelle Green

Coconut Shy, Ring Toss and Signs by Leeanne Bell.
Additional knitting by Michelle Green and Sally Bentham
Illustration of the village on page 2 by Carol Law

ABOUT SARAH

Sarah Simi was taught how to knit by her mum when she was eight. From then on, she was forever knitting jumpers, cuddly Clangers and even an outfit for her guinea pig that it sensibly refused to wear. After working as a stylist, designer and writer for many years, she collaborated with award-winning animator Ed Hartwell to make her first film, *nudinits – Tickled Pink*, which went on to win a Best Comedy Award and a Best Animation Award. They have since made more nudinit films and together own Woolly Vision, a stop-motion animation company specialising in using wool, fabric and felt. Sarah lives in Kent with her husband.

ABOUT CAROLINE

Caroline Bletsis is a professional knitter. Mainly self-taught, she started off by making outfits for her dolls and moved onto knitting Starsky-style chunky jackets as a teenager. She specialises in knitting the weird and wonderful: her work has included designing American university mascot scarves, miniature replicas of pet cats and dogs, as well as the huge array of incredible details featured in nudinits. Caroline lives with her family in Hampshire.

For my much better half, Roberto

First published in the United Kingdom in 2021 by
Collins & Brown
43 Great Ormond Street
London, WC1N 3HZ

An imprint of Pavilion Books Company Ltd

ISBN 978-1-911622-66-6

A CIP catalogue record for this book is available from the British Library.

10 9 8 7 6 5 4 3 2 1

Reproduction by Rival Colour Ltd, UK
Printed and bound by Toppan Leefung Printing Ltd, China

www.pavilionbooks.com